CONTENTS

Contents

PREFACE

Some explanation may be due about the need for this further contribution to an already voluminous literature on the subject. Most of the writing on development economics naturally has a specialist approach, and preaches to the converted in that it is addressed to an audience already very aware of the pressing nature of development problems. *Worlds Apart* aims at highlighting, for a wider and perhaps less committed readership, what surely must be the outstanding issue of our time – the already immense and rapidly widening gulf between the Rich and the Poor nations of the world. No economist can afford to miss an opportunity of communicating the urgent need to reverse forces which are dividing the world in two to an extent which is both morally intolerable and fraught with political implications which we may neglect at our peril.

The book grew out of my work for the BBC radio series 'Affluence and Inequality' first broadcast in the autumn of 1971. Its contents broadly follow the structure of the programmes. It attempts, first of all, to set the problem of underdevelopment in historical perspective – explaining the emergence of the 'development gap' and how it widened to its present alarming dimensions; the next two parts aim, in non-specialist terms, at distilling some of the basic economic analysis of underdevelopment – its symptoms, the technical problems faced by poor countries, and the international framework within which they have to solve them; finally, it stresses the need for *social* change and *political* will in achieving *economic* development.

My role in presenting the radio series was essentially one of linking information and various opinions on the subject into a meaningful whole; a book has a similar function but offers more scope for a personal interpretation and my own biases and feelings about development issues are very obvious from the text. *Worlds Apart* is not, however, offered as an original contribution to the subject, but merely as an attempt to emphasize questions which I believe to be of the very greatest urgency. The writing of this book has neatly spanned an already busy academic term, and I therefore gratefully confess the extent to which the work is derivative. The readers should also be warned of the need, in a short book dealing with a vast subject, for resort to considerable generalization and simplification of complex and controversial issues. My purpose will have been served if they are stimulated to read more widely about the subject and reach a standpoint from which they can make their own judgement.

My particular thanks are due to Betty Smith, research assistant in the BBC's education service, whom I duly exploited; to John Thomas, senior radio producer in the Further Education department, for both his discreet restraint in not telephoning to inquire about the book's progress and his invaluable last-minute editorial advice; to Hugh Purcell and David Dickinson, who produced the radio series with such care and sympathy; and to my colleague, Harold Pollins, who listened patiently and constructively. I am also grateful to my friend Geoffrey Ostergaard for pointing out that, with typical carelessness, I originally ascribed my closing quotation to Bakunin. It was, of course, Tolstoy who said: 'I sit on a man's back, choking him, and yet assure myself and others that I am very sorry for him and wish to ease his lot by any means possible, except getting off his back.'

Lastly, but most important, are Sheila – and Sally, Adam and Amanda – who suffered uncomplainingly my absences (and my presence) as only angels could.

PETER DONALDSON

PREFACE TO THE SECOND EDITION

Twelve years have passed since the first Penguin edition of *Worlds Apart*. They are years which have witnessed a dramatic shift in the balance of international economic power as a result of the concerted action by a group of oil-exporting countries. And they have also seen the emergence of a handful of Newly Industrialized Countries with rapidly expanding manufacturing sectors generally dominated by ever more powerful multinational companies in pursuit of their global strategies.

It has been a relatively difficult period for the Rich World – both because of these external pressures and because of its reaction to them in reverting to old-fashioned policy expedients of deflation. By the late 1970s there was talk of the end of an epoch. Could economic growth any longer be sustained? By the mid-1980s it seems more likely that the recession was only a hiccup in that process – but one which has left deep scars in the re-emergence of mass unemployment and deep social divisions.

For the greater part of the Poor World, little has changed during this period. The steady increase in the population in the Third World and the decline of population growth in the rich countries means that the proportion of people living in the underdeveloped nations is even greater now than a decade and a half ago. Profound inequalities persist and in some ways the plight of the poor has worsened. For example, the recession has exacerbated the international debt burden of Third World countries and led to demands for them to exercise 'disciplined' measures which may serve only to cripple their development prospects still further.

One encouraging sign is, I believe, that there is now a greater awareness of world poverty and a growing feeling among people in the richer nations that *something* should be done about it. Admittedly, this may often take the form of an emotional reaction to media coverage of horrendous famine or natural disasters in particular parts of the Third World. The next step is to ask how such situations can arise and to realize that they are only the grosser manifestations of a wider crisis. It is pleasing that today there are many more books like *Worlds Apart*, educational groups, television series and committed journalists aimed at helping those who are concerned to take that step.

In this revised edition I have retained the original structure and the basic arguments remain unchanged. Much has required up-dating, however, and in this process I have been very grateful for the highly professional assistance of John Tanner.

May 1985   PETER DONALDSON

PART ONE
WORLDS DRIFTING APART

Year by year the world becomes more sharply divided into two. On the one hand there are the advanced, industrial, developed, mature economies. And then there are the rest – developing, less developed, underdeveloped, undeveloped, pre-industrial or backward. The precise shade of euphemistic description is unimportant; for the basic division is, of course, one between Rich and Poor.

There have always been international economic inequalities, but never on the present scale. It is important to see the present economic gulf between nations in historical perspective for it is essentially a modern phenomenon, the product of roughly the last two hundred years. This very brief time span in the economic history of mankind has witnessed changes so profound as to render it radically different from all that had gone before.

What did go before? Basically, a precarious struggle between people and their environments, with sometimes the one getting on top and then the other. In Britain, for example, between the eleventh century and the seventeenth century, the prosperity or impoverishment of the economy depended crucially on the balance between the growth of population and the growth of food supplies.

In some periods, population growth outstripped the supply of food, in others there was a welcome breathing space.

The modern period, the last couple of centuries, is, in contrast, one in which for the first time output has consistently increased faster than population. What has made this possible is the process of *modern economic growth*. In most years, for over two centuries, Britain and the other now affluent countries have managed to increase the productive potential of their economies. They have enlarged their resources – by capital accumulation, the opening up of new territories, increased supplies of better quality labour, and additions to their stock of technical know-how; and they have learnt how to squeeze more output from those resources through increasingly efficient use. On a crude index, this has meant that in Britain, for instance, real incomes per head are now some seven or eight times greater than at the end of the seventeenth century.

Modern economic growth is unique in four respects:

(i) The present *level* of material affluence in rich economies is historically unprecedented.

(ii) Apart from occasional setbacks like those caused by the temporary oil price shocks in 1973 and 1979, the growth in output has been *sustained*. There were earlier episodes in which societies became temporarily richer, only to relapse after a while into their previous condition. Only in the modern period has output continued to increase, often unspectacularly but consistently, decade after decade. What makes present rich countries so affluent is not that they have grown so fast but that they have grown for a long time.

(iii) Growth is based in *exploding technologies*. We have experienced not just one, but a series of industrial revolutions – each containing the seeds of still more. The capacity has been created to produce and respond to one new technology after another.

(iv) Modern affluence is *dispersed*, permeating downwards through rich societies more than ever before. Greater dispersion does not necessarily mean greater equality, but the rich economies of today are, for the first time, based on *mass* consumption.

In all these ways, the economic history of the past few centuries has been very singular indeed. Surrendra J. Patel has strikingly summed up the economic achievement of an even shorter period, from 1850–1960, in the following way: 'If 6,000 years of man's "civilized" existence prior to 1850 is viewed as a day, the last 110 years is less than half an hour. But in that that "half-hour" of intense activity, more real output has been produced than during the preceding period. Over one third of the entire real income and about two thirds of the industrial output produced by mankind throughout its "civilized" history was generated in the industrial countries in the last century.'[1]

But if the occurrence of sustained economic growth has been confined to a very brief span of time, its incidence geographically has been equally narrow. It has been limited to only a handful of nations. Two thirds of the world has been passed by in the process – though far from unaffected by it. It is in these crucial few centuries that the present massive disparities between the income and wealth of rich and poor nations have developed.

In the mid eighteenth century, the world as a whole was economically much poorer. But the distribution of income and wealth between nations was then far more even. Some were richer than others, but seldom more than twice as rich. That is very different from the economic distance which now exists between the haves and the have-nots. International comparisons of income are notoriously suspect. But so long as we do not credit them with a spurious precision, they serve to give an idea of the order of magnitude involved. Britain may have been somewhat richer than India in the eighteenth century; its income per head is now roughly *thirty* times as great as that of India.

A further impression of how rapidly and radically the world economic scene has been transformed can be gleaned from Patel's heroic estimates of approximate changes in world distribution of population and income for the period 1850–1960.

This was a period in which world population increased two and a half times. But this was spectacularly exceeded by a ninefold expansion of world output. Those are the average figures, but when we break them down, we find that in the industrial countries, output increased some 2,000 per cent – while the increase in the pre-industrial nations was only about 300 per cent.

The consequence can be seen in the changed distribution

1. Patel, S. J., 'The Economic Distance between Nations: Its Origin, Measurement and Outlook', *Economic Journal*, March 1964.

1. Approximate changes in world distribution of population and income 1850–1960				
Areas	Population share in percentages		Income share in percentages	
	1850	1960	1850	1960
Industrial economies	26	28	35	78
Pre-industrial economies	74	72	65	22

Source: Patel, op. cit.

of income between the two groups. In 1850 the now industrial countries, with a quarter of the population, produced about one third of world output. By 1960 they accounted for no less than four fifths of world income. It is in this *very recent period* that international economic inequalities have grown to their present dimensions. What are the present facts of the matter?

The fact is that 74 per cent of the world's population had an income of less than £1,375 ($1,650) per annum in 1982. The fact is that the poorer half of the world's population had an income per head of less than £341 ($410) per annum. The fact is that 47 per cent of the world's population in the poorest countries earns only 5 per cent of the world's income, while the top 25 per cent of the world's population earns 79 per cent of world income.

The Rich and Poor continue to diverge. It is not difficult to see why. Suppose there are two countries, one with an income of $400 per capita and the other with $10,000 per capita – and that they both achieve a 2·5 per cent rate of growth in output per annum. What is the effect after one year?

2. Per capita income		
	Year 1	Year 2
Poor country	400	plus 2·5% growth	410
Rich country	10,000	plus 2·5% growth	10,250
Absolute gap	9,600		9,840

They both grow at the same rate, but the absolute gap between

Rich and Poor none the less widens. Indeed it would do so, for a while at least, even if the Poor managed to grow at *twice* the rate of the Rich.

3. Per capita income			
	Year 1		Year 2
Poor country	400	plus 5% growth	420
Rich country	10,000	plus 2·5% growth	10,250
Absolute gap	9,600		9,830

In this case, although the relative gap between the two has narrowed, the absolute gap continues to widen. If the Poor continued to grow at twice the rate of the Rich, the gap would ultimately be eliminated. But how long would it take?

(i) World Bank statisticians estimated the actual rate of growth per head in developing countries at only 2·1 per cent per annum for the period 1973–9. If that is all they can manage in the future, then the frightening fact is that it would take them no less than 176 years to catch up with the present British level of per capita income, and 191 years to achieve the present American level. And what would they find when they got there? The rich countries would not meanwhile have been standing still. They too would have been growing – and often at a faster rate. Inequality would have increased still further.

(ii) For some countries the question of catching up does not arise, either because their per capita growth rates are *less* than those of the rich economies or because their per capita income is actually *falling*. The GDP per person for the countries of Sub-Saharan Africa, for example, increased only slightly each year in the 1960s (an average of 1·3 per cent) and in the 1970s (an average of a mere 0·7 per cent a year). But in 1981 per capita income *fell* by 4 per cent, in 1982 by 3·3 per cent and in 1983 by an estimated 3·8 per cent.

The difference in output per head between the developed countries and the poor nations in 1982 amounted to over $10,000. On recent trends it will have widened to some $18,000 (at 1982 prices) even by the year 2000.

However, the most pressing problem for poor countries is not directly to do with the development gap. Their first objective must be to eliminate *absolute* poverty. But when this is achieved, attention will be focused still more clearly on the fact that there are two worlds. Poorer nations may well learn from the experience of richer ones that straightforward aping of their drive to high levels of material affluence brings costs and problems in its train. But they are unlikely to remain content with a situation of irrevocable and possibly growing disparities. For, although poor countries are those in which modern economic growth failed to take hold, they were none the less profoundly *affected* by it. The Rich World and Poor World today are joined by modern communications. No longer do the poor remain in blissful (or even miserable) ignorance of what is going on elsewhere. The cinema, radio and other mass media have opened the eyes of the poor two thirds of the world to the levels of affluence achieved elsewhere. Increasingly, they will demand their share of it. This is the so-called 'revolution of rising expectations'. Politicians, particularly of newly independent states, themselves imbued with a western optimism that economic problems are amenable to rational ordering, have promised greater prosperity. These hopes and ambitions are now reaching the masses – whose economic horizons, perhaps for the first time, now embrace the prospect of improvement. The consequences for the world of a failure to fulfil these newly aroused expectations are incalculable.

If the development gap is the product of only the last one or two hundred years, what needs explaining is how – from a not markedly different starting-point – some nations managed to pull away and achieve their present affluence. What lay behind this process which opened up the present massive gulf between Rich and Poor? The crux of the matter is not why most countries developed slowly – because that was the natural order of things. But rather, how did a handful of nations break through to a quite different plane of material opulence?

The answer lies in the process of modern economic growth – the ability of an economy to generate higher levels of output year after year. Incredibly it all started here in these islands. Mid-eighteenth-century Britain had slowly evolved to a point at which forces were set in motion which would radically transform its social and economic structure – and make it rich.

The first industrial revolution

Why, at that particular time, it happened to be Britain which was first to embark on the course of modern economic growth is a matter about which economic historians continue to wrangle. They argue about how the necessary conditions evolved and about their relative significance. But certainly by the latter part of the eighteenth century, all the ingredients for growth had emerged.

Britain was not specially blessed with natural resources. For example, the inputs for two of the major industries in the industrial revolution – cotton and iron – both had to be imported. But Britain did have sources of power, water to begin with and then coal. And it had relatively fertile land. This, coupled with an appropriate climate, proved vital. The agricultural transformation of the sixteenth and eighteenth centuries was crucial in a number of ways: in creating a food surplus to feed a non-agricultural population; in earning foreign exchange through exports; and in producing a surplus of capital accumulation which could be invested in other sectors of the economy.

Capital plays an important part in economic growth. A poor economy is one which consumes nearly all that it produces and perpetuates its poverty in the process. To do more than eke out a subsistence living, equipment is needed – machines, tools, buildings, roads and so on. But producing that equipment uses resources which might otherwise have been consumed. A poor economy has little to spare for capital accumulation. Britain, by the eighteenth century, *had* managed to generate such a surplus. Apart from that released by the growth of agricultural productivity, the main source of capital was the foreign trade sector – the fortunes built up by merchants engaged in the risky business of trading overseas. However, although achieving a surplus over current consumption was a necessary factor in the British economic miracle, the role of capital should not be exaggerated. Both the total and the rate of increase of capital were low.

Every schoolchild knows that the Britain of this time was the Britain of the steam engine, the spinning jenny, the crucible method of making steel and of all the other great inventions. And certainly the technological changes which were embodied in the growth of the capital stock during this period were vital for economic growth.

But many of the basic techniques which were now applied had in fact been invented much earlier. This was essentially a period of *innovation* in which the potential of past ideas was now realized. And the new techniques, although of utmost importance, could often hardly be classed as revolutionary. They were generally very simple improvements. Increased agricultural productivity, for example, was largely based on innovations like sowing seeds in straight lines, hoeing and the introduction of already known crop rotations. Similarly, in industry, improvements in machinery were thought up mostly by those who used them, rather than being the product of research based on scientific training. And so the new technology was one which was relatively easy to digest – which required little in the way of capital and work skills. For Britain, the problem of creating a new industrial workforce was not an acute one. No massive technical education programme was needed as a prerequisite of industrial development. The new techniques, because they were themselves unsophisticated and only gradually introduced, demanded relatively familiar, not alien, skills from those who operated them.

Another vital ingredient in the recipe for modern economic growth is the size of the market. Its importance lies in the fact, as Adam Smith put it, that 'the division of labour is limited by the extent of the market'. For it is its division of labour, its far greater degree of specialization, which perhaps above all distinguishes a rich economy from a poor one. And since specialization implies the trading of surpluses, development can be frustrated by inadequate opportunities for exchange. This could have been a serious problem for eighteenth-century Britain with a population of only six million – and that dispersed into fragmented markets by poor communications. It was of critical significance, therefore, that the industrial and agricultural revolutions were paralleled by the growth of coastal shipping; breakthroughs in road and bridge building; and, above all, by the creation of the canal system – to provide the basis for national markets. In addition, Britain, as a major world trader, could supplement its narrow domestic market by selling in the overseas territories which had been opened up during the preceding centuries.

Natural resources, a capital surplus, technology, appropriate labour supplies and a large enough market are all *necessary* conditions for economic growth, but they are not *sufficient*. Abundant resources or wide markets can remain unexploited; technical know-how is useless without innovation; surpluses of production over subsistence needs can be dissipated in ostentatious consumption, rather than salted away in productive investment.

What is also called for is the organizational facility to combine them effectively. Principally this is a matter of what economists call 'entrepreneurship' – decision-taking ability in conditions of risk. Entrepreneurship involves a drive for material success, a willingness to seek out opportunities to achieve it, and an ability to exploit those opportunities. In Britain there emerged a breed of small producers looking for ways to invest their capital profitably and keen to multiply their profits by ploughing them back into further expansion.

The origin of this entrepreneurial spirit in Britain is a matter of sociological speculation. There are those who stress the initiative bred of the nuclear rather than extended family system – coupled with a system of primogeniture which made for both the preservation of wealth accumulated generation by generation and the availability of younger sons forced to establish themselves in other fields. There is a school of thought which identifies the Protestant Ethic, with its emphasis on individual moral responsibility, as the source of capitalist drive. Saving – the preservation rather than dissipation of the fruits of industry; hard work – to exploit fully God-given talents; self-help for the poor. These were the paths of moral righteousness – and, fortuitously, the road to economic development. Everett Hagen, on the other hand, has argued that entrepreneurship results from the existence of outgroups in society denied the conventional channels of enhancing their status.[2] On this view, English non-conformists, conscious of their rejection by established society, were forced to look for fulfilment in other directions – and providently found them in growth-orientated business enterprise.

Whatever their origin, the entrepreneurs were at hand as a catalyst to activate the other elements in the growth process. A climate of economic change was created in which, to use Professor Rostow's expression, 'growth impulses were finally released and

2. Hagen, E. E., *On the Theory of Social Change*, Tavistock Publications, 1964.

traditional blockages to development were finally overcome'. It
was not something which happened overnight. Some historians are
wedded to Rostow's notion of a 'take-off' into sustained economic
growth – with its suggestion that the process is one of discrete
change.[3] In fact what took place in Britain was of an evolutionary
rather than a revolutionary nature, with long-term forces gradually
coming to a boil. What emerged, nevertheless, was a society
fundamentally different in its structure and attitudes from that of
a century or two earlier. Economic horizons became increasingly
widened. People began to see prospects of change and improvement
and were no longer necessarily resigned to the lot of their parents
and grandparents. They could start to think in terms of their
children doing better than themselves.

This is not the place to go into the details of how Britain was
transformed from a traditional and rather static agrarian society
into a growing industrial economy. But three fundamental features
of the change are worth emphasizing.

The first is that although Britain was the first to undergo the
process of modern economic growth (and partly, indeed, *because*
it was the first), development at that time was in many ways easier
than it is for poor countries today. The amount of new skills, capital
and technical change needed to set the ball rolling were not very
great. This was only the beginning and for the beginning only
marginal adjustments were needed, releasing forces which would
then become cumulative in their impact. And the required changes
were not radically alien to the comprehension of a traditional
society. They were comparatively easy to initiate and digest.

A second salient feature of British development was its painful-
ness. The costs of change were enormous. In the end, the agricultural and industrial transformation of Britain led to vast
improvements in the standard of living of the mass of British
people. But there was a marked short-term deterioration in their
lot. Admittedly, this is a controversial area. Per capita income
actually rose during the industrial revolution. But how much of
this was illusory? How much of this increase was merely existing
output being brought for the first time under the measuring rod of
money? And how much increased output, like that stemming from

3. Rostow, W. W., *The Stages of Economic Growth*, CUP, 1960.

transport and other urban expenditures, should more properly be
counted as a cost rather than a benefit of economic expansion?
Then again, the evidence suggests that the 'quality of life' was
deteriorating – in terms of dietary standards, the growing congestion and squalor of town life, the misery and danger and insecurity
of work in the new factories. Above all, there were the incalculable
costs of the disruption of a traditional society. This was 'sacrificial'
development – with what contemporary commentators like John
Stuart Mill or Lord John Russell regarded as intolerable burdens
being imposed on immediate generations in order that subsequent
ones would benefit. The popular conception of the mechanism by
which recent communist economies have developed thus turns out
to be the path which we ourselves travelled.

   In Britain, of course, this was not the result of deliberate strategic
decisions taken from above. British development was spontaneous
and unplanned. This made the process both socially more agonizing
and, in some respects, relatively easier to accomplish. Rapid industrialization took place free from externally imposed constraints
of social justice. Few obligations were placed on employers to
safeguard the welfare of their workers. Their profits were untouched by taxes to provide social services or to meet the costs of
the urban nightmares created by their industrial complexes. They
were left to get on with the job of maximizing profits – and therefore,
it was hoped, social gain as well – solely on the basis of what
appeared in their own balance sheets.

   In view of all this – a remarkably favourable conjunction of
growth elements and a political and social climate in which energies
could be channelled uninhibitedly into single-minded striving for
maximizing the rate of growth – the British achievement, in hard
terms, turns out to be surprisingly slight. This is the third aspect of
British development which needs stressing. The growth rate during
the nineteenth century, when Britain had a head start, was *not*
spectacular. 'If total national product grew between 2 and 3 per
cent per annum over most of the nineteenth century (then) product
per head grew by only about 1·5 per cent in the first half of the
century and by less than 2·5 per cent for most of the second half.'[4]
   During the postwar period in Britain there has been widespread

4. Deane, P., *The First Industrial Revolution*, CUP, 1965, p. 274.

despondency about our poor economic record. But during these years, the growth rate per capita has been higher than we achieved in the heyday of early industrialization. The growth rate then managed by Britain is even less impressive when compared with the record of subsequent high fliers like Japan or the Soviet Union. And it is as nothing compared with what present poor countries feel that they must now achieve to cope with their problems of relative and absolute poverty.

The point is, of course, that the British economic expansion was sustained for a very long period of time. The base from which Britain started, coupled with the maintenance of a quite modest economic growth rate over a couple of centuries, has been sufficient to make ours one of the most affluent societies of today. Britain, first in the field, could afford such a timespan. Poor countries today can't. And it is depressing from their point of view that Britain, with all its advantages, did not manage a more dramatic development than it did.

Modern economic growth, having begun in Britain, subsequently spread to other parts of the world – but only to that handful of countries which today comprise the rich world. Growth spread to Europe and to lands settled from Europe. And that was nearly the extent of it. Until very recently, apart from exceptional cases like Japan, modern economic growth was an almost exclusively European phenomenon.

European countries

The first industrial revolution might have taken place in any of a number of West European countries. With broadly similar cultures and being closely linked geographically and socially, they sooner or later followed the British example. The different time lags between British development and theirs can largely be explained by the relative ease or difficulty with which each of them overcame some special blockage or forged some missing link which had prevented them from being first in the field.

Growth took firm hold in Germany, for example, only in the last three decades of the nineteenth century – and this was mainly because, until 1871, Germany consisted of loosely connected independent states. It was estimated that in 1790, between them, there were no less than three hundred separate tax authorities and eighteen hundred customs boundaries. And, although the commercial unification of Prussia and the creation of the 1834 Zollverein – a customs union of eighteen states – did much to stimulate manufacturing and commerce by a widening of markets, Germany remained seriously fragmented by a transport system which contained, for instance, sixty-seven different railway authorities each setting its own rates. Thus, although a start was made in agricultural and industrial development before political unity was finally established, its pace was limited until the formation of the German Reich in 1871. This done, however, Germany had little difficulty in catching up with Britain. The gap between them was never more than a generation or two – very different from the situation of poor countries today.

Like the British, French development was evolutionary and, indeed, even less dramatic. The main reasons for slower French economic growth appear to have been sociological. Despite the upheavals of 1789 and after, traditional values remained deeply entrenched and continued to reflect the ethos of the aristocracy: land ownership as the basic status symbol, cultivation of a sophisticated non-material outlook, and a general contempt for those who made their way through commercial and industrial activities. In addition, limited markets – due to a highly unequal income distribution – and the cautious conservatism bred in the family business structure, have been stressed as further retarding factors. France drifted into the growth process none the less – but without, in the nineteenth century, much drive or dynamism.

The Russian case is an example of those European countries which were initially left behind in the growth race. Partly this was due to an inadequate infrastructure (particularly of transport and communications) but principally it was because of the feudal nature of Russian society, stifling of individual initiative and difficult to gear towards growth-orientation. The beginnings of Russian growth in the latter part of the nineteenth century had a certain artificiality. Conditions conducive to growth were deliberately stimulated by the government rather than emerging spontaneously as elsewhere. Early Russian development was highly paternalistic and leaned heavily on foreign capital and expertise. It was also spasmodic, and how far it had become self-sustaining by the

beginning of the First World War we shall never know. The
breakdown of the economy during the war meant that the revolutionary regime effectively had to start again from scratch. In
doing so, it set the pattern for those other European countries
which had missed the mainstream of the growth breakthrough and
which tended, in their efforts to make good the leeway, to pursue
a strategy of rapid, planned, capital accumulation and a build-up of
a heavy industrial base through an initial restraint of consumption.

Thus, between European countries there were important differences which explain the varied timing of their transformations. But
the underlying similarity of their social and economic structures,
their attitudes and endowments, meant that in the end they all
moved on to the same path of modern economic growth.

Lands of European settlement

This was the second group of countries to which the growth process
spread. They were the newly opened lands peopled by European
immigrants. Between 1850 and 1890, from Britain one and a
quarter million people left for the United States, Canada, Australia
and New Zealand. These were countries in which a fresh start
could be made; and because they were settler societies (with the
indigenous populations largely eliminated), there were fewer traditional blockages to development like those back home. There
were three chief factors in their success stories. They had an
abundance of natural resources. They were peopled by immigrants
who tended to possess, *a fortiori*, those growth-orientated attitudes
which were coming to characterize the societies from which they
were drawn. And finally, they were helped by capital and trade
flows from the metropolitan countries.

About the classic case of American development, Professor
Richard T. Gill has commented that 'it is doubtful whether quite
such opportune conditions for achieving economic development
have occurred in any other country in the world, before or since'.[5]
It would have been astonishing only had development *not* taken
hold. In the first place, America was endowed massively with land,
minerals and climatic variety. On top of this, it had the rich stock
of human capital embodied in its wholly imported population – a

5. Gill, R. T., *Economic Development: Past and Present*, Prentice-Hall, 1967.

population which had been educated and trained at the metropolitan countries' expense, and which tended to have just those qualities – youth, initiative and thirst for success – which make for the entrepreneurial drive which is one of the more elusive elements of the development mechanism. And, since labour was in relatively short supply, there was an emphasis right from the start on mechanization, the substitution of capital for labour whenever possible. Finally, the American population was more homogeneous than that of the Old World. With lesser income disparities and a willingness to submerge old identities in the new American nationality, there was a tendency towards conformism in consumption patterns which served as a base for standardization and the economies of mass production techniques. Because the environment in which it was cultured was even more favourable than that of the metropolitan countries, there was in American development an air of easy inevitability.

Japan

This is the exception to the almost exclusively European history of economic growth until very recent times. In this highly singular case of oriental economic development there is a crucial date – 1868. Before 1868 Japan had been a feudal regime deliberately isolated, through the Seclusion Edicts, from foreign trade and any other contact with the outside world. Foreign powers, particularly America and Russia, were anxious to gain entry to the Japanese market and they finally succeeded in shattering its seclusion. This enforced exposure, in humiliating circumstances – and partly as a result of demonstrably superior European techniques – was a major factor in the downfall of the old Tokugawa regime and the restoration of the Emperor Meiji in 1868. From then on, Japanese policy was completely reversed – to create maximum exposure to western influences. The government gave every encouragement to foreign entrepreneurs and technical collaborators. The Japanese themselves were stimulated to go abroad and acquire modern expertise. Efforts were made to induce home industry to adopt western methods, the government itself importing machinery and goods to stimulate import substitutes. Western know-how was disseminated through technical colleges, travelling teachers and industrial fairs. In all this, the role of the government was crucial.

As G. C. Allen put it, 'there was scarcely any Japanese industry of
the Western type ... which did not owe its establishment to State
initiative'.[6] And, as a source of domestic capital, there was the
agricultural sector – with the peasant being mercilessly squeezed
by highly regressive taxation into greater efficiency. In growth
terms, it paid off, with the textile industry providing the first leading
sector.

The quite exceptional nature of the Japanese case needs stressing
once again. On the one hand there was the highly strategic role of
the State – motivated in this case by 'reactive nationalism' –
ruthlessly seeking economic efficiency, to achieve political and
military parity with the nations by which Japan had previously
been humiliated. And, on the other hand, there was the degree to
which the Japanese peasantry was prepared to accept the burden
of growth through punitive taxation and restricted consumption.
The extent to which the State was able to pursue this sacrificial
strategy can perhaps only be fully explained in terms of the cultural
inheritance of the Japanese themselves and the degrading historical
episodes which preceded the beginnings of modern economic
growth in Japan.

Britain, Europe, lands of European settlement and Japan – that
was the extent to which the growth process spread. Why was
modern economic growth almost wholly confined to Europe and
countries peopled from Europe? In examining the origin of the
development gap, we must ask why it was that the other two thirds
of the world failed to undergo similar changes *at that time*. All that
can be done here is to indicate briefly three broad factors working
to create an initial economic inequality between nations.

(i) *Difference in natural environment*. The narrow geographic
incidence of modern affluence certainly suggests that natural environmental differences may have some part to play in explaining
disparities in economic development. Modern economic growth
has largely taken place in temperate parts of the world. It is the
tropical, equatorial and sub-temperate zones in which most of the
poor countries are situated.

6. Allen, G. C., *Short Economic History of Modern Japan*, Allen & Unwin, 2nd
edn, 1962.

Why should extreme climates tend to impede economic development? Well, first of all, lands in such zones are often relatively infertile. Although, in the case of equatorial regions, luxuriant rain forests may give an impression to the contrary, the soil is frequently poor. Infertility, coupled with the natural difficulties of cultivating such areas, meant that life in, for example, eighteenth-century African countries was very hard indeed. Low agricultural productivity prevented the emergence of a surplus of production over and above subsistence requirements, a surplus on which development could be based. Then again, in hot regions, weeds, pests and disease tend to proliferate more easily – simultaneously increasing the difficulty of successful cultivation and sapping human capacity to deal with the task (although there is no real evidence that extreme climates, in themselves, reduce willingness to work). Finally, the non-temperate regions of the world have frequently been characterized by fragmentation, either because harsh conditions were capable of supporting only sparse populations so that communities were relatively isolated from each other, or because natural barriers – forests, rivers, mountains – impeded communications. From the point of view of economic development these are serious obstacles – in limiting the size of markets and restricting the diffusion of know-how and the interchange of ideas. Eighteenth-century Europe, in contrast, was a relatively compact region of closely linked communities.

(ii) *Cultural differences.* Is the truth of the matter that, superimposed on its environmental advantages (and partly perhaps determined by its natural endowments), European culture *was* peculiarly orientated towards economic development – while that of others was simply lacking in this respect? Put in its most objectionable form, this argument suggests that the European had the energy, drive and achievement-motivation to become economically successful, while non-European societies have been marked by economic inertia – a reluctance to work and lack of interest in material gain. Generations of colonial administrators, despairing at the indolence of their primitive native subjects, doubtless subscribed to this view – more recently re-stated by a Dutch economist, Professor J. H. Boeke, in his theory of social dualism.[7] Boeke's

7. Boeke, J. H., *Economics and Economic Policy of Dual Societies*, Inst. of Pacific Relations, 1953.

thesis is that eastern societies are profoundly biased towards limited wants, lack of interest in risk-bearing and economic advancement – of responses so radically different from those of the West that the possibility of modern economic growth simply does not exist.

Of course, even if it were true that these substantial cultural *differences* obtained, it would be quite unjustifiable to jump to the conclusion that European society was culturally *superior*. Recent research has revealed the immense cultural richness and diversity of societies which were economically hard-pressed; but the crux of the matter is whether, in any case, the distinction between eastern and western societies is a valid one. *If* it is true that economic responses in the former were sluggish or perverse, what would that show? Since most of the observations to that effect were made in countries administered by metropolitan powers, does it tell us anything other than that *opportunities* for material advancement under such a system were limited? The evidence accumulated by researchers such as P. T. Bauer[8] suggests that, where the opportunities exist, individuals in less developed economies are as quick to seize them as their western counterparts – as profit-seeking, avaricious and materialistic.

However, it is probably true that at the time when present rich countries were beginning to embark on the process of modern economic growth, a large group of countries were not in a position to follow suit – they lacked one or more of the necessary ingredients of economic development. Partly this was the result of environmental factors already mentioned, coupled with isolation from the forces taking hold elsewhere. But it was also partly due to the fact that many of them were already gripped in a system of formal or informal colonialism.

(iii) *The colonial framework*. A large part of the now less developed world was, at the time when now rich countries began to develop, subordinate to a handful of metropolitan powers – whether that was formalized into colonial status or whether they were merely in a sphere of influence so strong that formal annexation was unnecessary. How far was *this* the reason for the emergence of an initial economic inequality between nations?

8. Bauer, P. T., and Yamey, B. S., *The Economics of Underdeveloped Countries*, Nisbet, 2nd edn, 1970.

There were different aspects of the relationship. There was, first of all, 'blood and plunder' imperialism, with the centre powers exacting primitive tribute from their satellites. During the eighteenth century, for example, some three million slaves were transported in British ships at a profit of £20–£30 per head, and there was the straightforward booty such as that drained from India after the Battle of Plassey in 1757. But it is doubtful if crude imperialism such as this did much to establish an initial development gap. 'Commercial' gains of this kind were more attractive than risky industrial enterprise and this was the period, in Britain, of the nabobs returned from their foreign exploits setting themselves up in ostentatious splendour rather than engaging in entrepreneurial activity.

An interesting aspect of the imperial relationship is that, to begin with, the overseas areas were regarded as sources of exotic consumer goods which could not be produced at home. This stemmed not only from different climatic conditions as in the case of spices, but also because of the *technological superiority* of overseas producers in certain lines of production. Indian textiles, for example, were greatly in demand in eighteenth-century Britain because British producers lacked the technical know-how to produce goods of such sophisticated design and material – and cheapness. Imperialism in this period, therefore, took the form of establishing and keeping open the trading links of the great trading monopolies like the East India Company. Apart from keeping out other powers, the imperial interest dictated merely that the goods should be carried in British ships – and this was achieved through the old Navigation Acts.

However, once the British industrial revolution began to take place, the British interest markedly changed. The activities of the East India Company, far from providing a welcome supplement to the deficiencies of the British industrial system, were now seen as a direct threat to its development. How could the emergent British textile and metallurgy industries, for example, ever hope to get off the ground in the face of competition from the technically superior Indian producers? The answer was that the latter, and the East India Company, had to be broken. In the event, 75 per cent duties on imports from India proved necessary to do the job: but the job was done thoroughly. Within a few decades the flow of goods from India to Britain had been replaced by traffic in the opposite direction. In the twenty years after 1814, British cotton manufactured exports to India increased from a million yards to fifty-one million. Similar increases took place in exports of wool, iron, pottery, glass and paper. The concomitant was the destruction of Indian producers. Indian cotton exports shrank from a million and a quarter pieces in 1814 to sixty-three thousand, thirty years later. As Michael Barratt Brown puts it, 'the population of Dacca, Surat and Murshidibad and other centres for manufacture in India was decimated in a generation'.[9]

So here was a case in which, during a short but crucial phase of its own development, the imperial power – through protection of its domestic industry – killed off actual and potential competition from the periphery. It was a tactic which Britain tried to employ in other cases too, but not always with the same success. Strenuous efforts were made, for example, to prevent the emergence of an industrial sector in the American colonies. Export of machinery and designs, and the setting up of blast furnaces there, were all made illegal. But to no avail: because the American colonies fought for, and won, their independence rather than accept such constraints on their development. *They* were strong enough to achieve it. Others were not; and there is no doubt that colonialism was a factor impeding the growth of now poor economies. *How* significant it was in creating the initial inequality between nations depends on whether the peripheral countries would have developed anyway. Perhaps some of them would, but there were others, for reasons which we have already suggested, which would certainly have not – *at that time*.

But that is not the end of the imperial story. If imperialism was only partly responsible for creating an initial equality, it certainly then worked to *widen* the development gap. In a variety of ways, it prevented the emergence, in economically more backward areas, of those conditions necessary for economic development.

Thus one major factor preventing development in the colonial areas was the commercial policy of the metropolitan powers. The way in which *trade* served to widen an initial economic inequality can again be illustrated by the British case. By the thirties and the

9. Brown, M. Barratt, *After Imperialism*, Heinemann, 1963, p. 47.

forties of the nineteenth century, the industrial revolution had gathered momentum. The possibilities of industrial competition from the colonies had, as we have already seen, been effectively prevented by the destruction of their industries through high tariffs. At this stage there was a dramatic reversal in Britain's external commercial policy. Behind it lay the growing strength of the manufacturing interest, the so-called 'Manchester School' – arguing that restrictive protectionism was no longer required. What this vocal and powerful pressure group demanded was a dismantling of those barriers to trade which had been appropriate at an earlier stage and the creation of a free trade environment in which they were confident that they could now flourish.

The prospect of free trade was an attractive one for a number of reasons. Firstly, because it meant cheap food. Britain was becoming more and more dependent on imported foodstuffs – but British farmers remained protected against foreign competition through the Corn Laws. However, what was good for agriculture was bad for the manufacturers. For them, dear food pushed up wage costs – and this meant higher manufacturing prices. Similarly, industrial expansion in a country as sparsely endowed with natural resources as Britain required a large volume of raw materials to be imported from abroad. Once again the manufacturing interest lay in obtaining them as cheaply as possible. Finally, foreign trade was seen by the manufacturers as a vital way of supplementing a still small home market.

For all these reasons, they argued in favour of free trade; and they won the day. In 1845 the Corn Laws were repealed, followed later by the cumbersome Navigation Acts. Restrictions were swept away and Britain embarked on nearly a century of free trade during which British markets were open to all-comers and policy was aimed at establishing a similar state of affairs throughout the world as a whole. To understand how this basic switch in British policy worked to widen the development gap, a brief digression is needed into the economics of free trade.

The economics of free trade

The move to free trade was endorsed by the weight of received economic thinking of the time, exemplified in particular in the writings of David Ricardo. Economic theory suggested that free trade, the maximization of the international exchange of goods, was in the interest not only of British manufacturers, but also of the rest of the world.

Domestically, the most powerful single factor increasing the wealth of the community had been the increased division of labour. The breakthrough to increased output stemmed primarily from increasing specialization – first of all by product, and subsequently by process. By specializing in this way, and then exchanging the consequent surpluses, a far larger quantity and range of output had been made possible.

The free trade economists of the nineteenth century merely extended this reasoning to the international economy. In the same way that individuals are born with and develop quite different talents and aptitudes, so countries are also endowed with very different quantities and qualities of resources, labour and capital. Rather than try to produce all their own requirements domestically, it pays them to concentrate on those lines at which they are best and to exchange their surpluses for goods which can be produced more cheaply elsewhere.

But suppose that Britain can produce *everything* more cheaply than, say, France. Surely the theory breaks down at this point: specialization and trade will benefit neither of the countries? On the contrary, argued Ricardo, it will still be to the advantage of *both*. He emphasized that the basis for specialization lay in *comparative*, and not absolute, advantage. Even if Britain *could* produce everything more cheaply than France, there will be some types of production in which its superiority is *most* marked; and it will pay Britain to shift resources into those lines of production and to use the resulting increase in output to buy from France goods in which the British superiority is less significant. The doctor who is a better typist than his secretary none the less finds it pays to employ her because it enables him to concentrate on medicine – in which his advantage over his secretary is far greater.

This, then, was the classical argument for free trade. Only if prices were undistorted by artificial barriers to trade would they reflect the underlying cost of production. Only then would international specialization be fully extended; and the benefits of increased economic efficiency would accrue to all those taking part –

whether they were initially rich or poor, or whatever their natural endowments.

Economic thinking of the early nineteenth century thus provided a powerful rationale for the British conversion to free trade. Sweeping away barriers to trade would benefit not only Britain itself, but also the rest of the world.

Effects of free trade – for Britain

Between 1840 and 1874, world trade grew some 500 per cent and, of the total, Britain was involved in no less than two fifths. British exports expanded at an astonishing rate and found their way, particularly textiles, into every market of the world. Imports grew correspondingly. In the 1850s and 1860s no less than one third of the rest of the world's exports came to Britain.

Britain opened wide its own markets and those of its colonies; and the further expansion of the Empire which took place in the nineteenth century was sometimes dictated by the wish to prevent other powers from moving in – powers whose interest might be to keep their new-found markets closed to outsiders. Britain's imperial aim was to open up those markets; at this stage of supremacy there was no need to fear the effects of competition.

Trade followed the flag; and not far after trade came overseas investment. By 1850 the British stake in overseas economies amounted to some £250 million. By the First World War the extent of British overseas assets had increased to nearly £4,000 million. By that time, indeed, the annual net amount being invested abroad was three times the amount being put into British domestic industry itself. The feedback from this vast build-up of overseas capital was of enormous importance. Directly it led to increased demand for British capital goods exports – for railways, heavy engineering goods, and the like. Britain supplied the finance and the money was spent on British goods. And, indirectly, as such investment led to the opening up and development of new territories, the market for exports of British consumer goods subsequently expanded too. Finally, as British capital accumulation overseas increased, so did the return flow to Britain of profits, interest and dividends on that investment – a flow of great significance for the balance of payments.

Thus, for Britain, the gains from free trade were enormous: a vast extension of the domestic market to sustain the pace of British industrial development; a source of cheap inputs of raw materials and foodstuffs; and the establishment of Britain as a colossal world creditor nation. But what of Britain's trading partners?

The effects of free trade on the rest of the world

Implicit in the classical free trade argument was the notion that what was good for Britain was good for the world. The benefits of specialization and trade would accrue to all the partners in the enterprise. To some extent this is what in fact happened.

But free trade was established within the framework of an initial inequality between nations (which was itself partly due to a protectionist policy aimed at destroying overseas competition to the new British growth industries). Free trade and competition was therefore between highly unequal partners. Although both rich and poor perhaps gained from the process as free trade economists predicted they would, those gains were very unequally distributed; and there were also profoundly injurious long-term effects on the less developed economies.

The pattern of specialization which would take place between the metropolitan and dependent territories was obvious. Here was Britain, the first industrial power – the workshop of the world – in which the secrets of manufacturing industry had been learned and applied. And here, on the other hand, were colonial countries in which any embryo industries had already been destroyed – but which possessed mineral and climatic endowments which the mother country lacked. Clearly, Britain should concentrate on making manufactured goods and export them in exchange for primary products – foodstuffs and raw materials. Such specialization would be mutually beneficial and frictionless too, since the output of the colonial territories was complementary to, rather than competitive with, that of the mother country. It seemed a natural division of labour.

But how natural was it in fact? Since, as was stressed earlier, it was the tropical colonial countries which tended to be less well endowed agriculturally, might a 'natural' division of labour not have been the opposite of what had taken place? It can be argued that the long-run comparative advantage of the now rich countries actually lay in primary production, but that *this* pattern of specialization failed to emerge – in some cases because the now poor countries were not at that time ripe for industrialization – and in others because industrialization was stifled at birth by colonial protectionism.

A classic division of labour between primary and secondary producers is, in any case, likely to lead to an unequal distribution of the gains from trade. Productivity in agriculture is harder to increase than that of manufacturing industry, principally because of the greater opportunities for exploiting economies of large-scale production and technical advance which exist in the manufacturing sector. For these and other reasons which will be touched upon later,[10] a forced dependence on agricultural production worked over the years to widen the gap between rich and poor countries.

But what of the massive British investment overseas? That certainly might have contributed towards preparing the ground for the development of the poorer regions; but by and large it failed to do so. The great part of that investment was directed into other already developing areas and the 'White Dominions'. To the extent that capital flowed to the poorer colonial territories at all, it tended to be concentrated in the mining and plantation sectors of their economies, leading only to 'enclave' development. The capital, techniques and skilled personnel were all imported from the investing country with the recipient economy providing only the unskilled labour. Consequently, the 'spread' effects of such investment were negligible. Profits were repatriated; there was little demand generated for local products; and there was only limited 'learning effect' from the use of superior techniques. The enclave was an extension of the investor's domestic economy, rather than the basis of wider development in the recipient country. The result was the creation of 'dualism', the uneasy co-existence of modern and traditional economic sectors – causing problems which continue to plague less developed countries today.

It is not easy to draw up a balance sheet for imperialism. If it imposed an artificial and, in the long run, unfair division of labour, and if it bred an unhealthy enclave type of development, there were also ways in which it worked to the *benefit* of the colonial territories. The period of colonial rule was one in which the colonies were

10: See Part Four, I, *Unfair Exchange?*, p. 108.

exposed to outside ideas and influences; their markets were widened and integrated to a greater degree than ever before; there was a build-up of roads, railways, bridges and other infrastructure investment; and it was a period in which law and order was imposed and the basis laid of sound administration. But against these benefits, it can be argued that imperialism inculcated in the subordinate territories attitudes resistant to the changes required for modern economic growth. Partly this was just a reinforcement of existent indigenous tendencies. The imperialist powers often bought themselves security by supporting feudal aristocracies which controlled the colonial domains – elitist groups which were doing and continued to do very well out of the system as it stood and who therefore had a vested interest against the process of change. Often, too, the attitudes of the rulers rubbed off on the ruled. Unfortunately, the values which were thus imbibed were not those on which the British economic revolution had been based – of thriftiness, hard work and entrepreneurial drive. The values displayed in the imperial shop window were those of the Raj – ostentatious consumption, gentlemanly disdain for hard work, and administrative caution. Attitudes such as these often still prevail in poor countries today and lead to misguided attempts at emulative rather than genuinely indigenous development.

The gap between rich and poor countries steadily widened. And, at least in the case of British imperialism, the mechanism by which it did so was not primarily that of crude exploitative exaction of colonial tribute. It happened through the application of an apparently 'fair' system of free trade – which could be defended as being in the interest of all concerned. In fact, all *may* have benefited, but none more than Britain itself with its industrial headstart. Having established an initial advantage over other producers, Britain could afford to throw open its markets to the rest of the world and lure or instruct them to do the same. Free trade could be relied upon to do the rest.

PART TWO
SYMPTOMS OF UNDERDEVELOPMENT

1. What it means to be poor

It has always been advantageous to be born on the right side of the fence. But the accident of birth has never had quite the far-reaching significance which it holds today. For every child produced to parents in the developed countries, eight are now born in the underdeveloped world. This fact, above all else, will determine the course of their lives. The chances are that most of the eight will be born and brought up in poverty. Poverty, however difficult it is to define and measure, is the normal condition of mankind; it is the lucky few in the developed countries who are the exception rather than the rule.

What does it mean to be born poor? It means, first of all, that during your working life you will produce little by way of output, and earn little in the way of income. In 1982, output per head in the United States worked out at $13,160 – for every man, woman and child. In Britain the figure was $9,660, in Mexico $2,270, in Kenya $390, in Ghana $360, in Sri Lanka $320, in India only $260.

International comparisons of income and output such as those

4. Gross National Product per capita, 1984 (US dollars)			
Switzerland	17,010	Malaysia	1,860
Saudi Arabia	16,000	Jordan	1,690
Sweden	14,040	Paraguay	1,610
USA	13,160	Turkey	1,370
Denmark	12,470	Jamaica	1,330
Canada	11,320	Peru	1,310
Australia	11,140	Zimbabwe	850
Japan	10,080	Zambia	640
UK	9,660	Bolivia	570
New Zealand	7,920	Kenya	390
Israel	5,090	Pakistan	380
Venezuela	4,140	Ghana	360
Argentina	2,520	Sri Lanka	320
Mexico	2,270	Tanzania	280
Brazil	2,240	India	260
Chile	2,210	Uganda	230
South Korea	1,910	Ethiopia	140

Source: World Bank, World Development Report, 1984, OUP, 1984

in table 4 are only a crude index of the economic disparities
between nations and of the poverty of those at the lower end of
the scale. Millions of people do somehow manage to subsist on
desperately low incomes which would make even minimal physical
survival in Western Europe or North America well-nigh impossible. For a variety of technical reasons, we cannot draw the obvious
conclusions from the figures – that the average American, for
instance, is more than fifty times better off than the average Indian.
National income comparisons give an idea of the broad magnitude
of the different economic levels of rich and poor countries, but
beyond that we must proceed cautiously. Some of the problems
involved in interpreting such statistics are touched upon in a later
section.

One of the first problems of being born poor is how to survive
infancy (table 5). In Britain, ninety-nine children of every hundred
born are still alive on their first birthday. But nine Indian babies

5. Infant mortality rate per 1,000 births					
Japan	7	United Arab Emirates	50	India	94
UK	11	Philippines	51	Burma	96
USA	11	Colombia	54	Tanzania	98
Poland	20	Syria	58	Indonesia	102
Chile	27	Brazil	73	Algeria	111
Sri Lanka	32	Peru	83	Bangladesh	133

Source: ibid.

out of every hundred never reach that age. Twelve of every hundred born in Ethiopia die in their first year of life.

Being born poor, the chances are that you will spend your life being rather hungry. Estimates suggest that between one tenth and one fifth of the world's population is suffering from malnutrition. Nutrition experts regard a dietary intake of 2,500 calories a day as a basic requirement for proper health. Table 6 shows the very different standards of diet which are typical in rich countries and in poor countries.

6. Daily calorie supply per capita, 1981			
USA	3,647	Brazil	2,529
UK	3,322	Colombia	2,521
Egypt	2,941	Algeria	2,433
South Korea	2,931	Nigeria	2,361
Syria	2,908	Philippines	2,318
Mexico	2,805	Peru	2,183
Iran	2,795	Kenya	2,056
Chile	2,790	Ghana	1,995
Japan	2,740	Tanzania	1,985
Ivory Coast	2,670	India	1,906

Source: ibid.

Inadequate dietary standards are a major contributory factor to yet another dimension of poverty – the high incidence of disease: '... nutritional deficiency is serious not only because it lowers resistance to disease, and permits a high incidence in poor countries of, for example, kwashiorkor; malnutrition can also cause severe brain damage to young children. It has been calculated that the brain reaches 90 per cent of its normal structural development in the first four years of life, and it is known that during this critical period the brain is highly vulnerable to nutritional deficiencies; such deficiencies can cause as much as 25 per cent impairment of normal mental ability, and a deterioration of only 10 per cent is enough seriously to handicap productive life.'[1] But on the other hand, this is one area in which enormous progress has been made during the postwar period. The transmission of medical technology to poor countries has been dramatically effective in reducing the incidence of some endemic diseases. The last smallpox case, for example, was recorded in Somalia in October 1977. Infant death rates have been halved in the last twenty years.

7. Infant mortality rates (deaths per 1,000 live births)		
	1960	1982
Low income developing countries	165	87
Middle income developing countries	126	76
Western industrial nations	29	10
Eastern Europe	36	21
Source: ibid.		

Individual medical care, however, remains hopelessly inadequate. Table 8 gives an indication of your chances, if you happen to live in a poor country, of visiting a doctor or receiving hospital treatment.

Born poor, the likelihood is that you will be ill-educated or even unable to read and write. Tables 9 and 10 give UNESCO and World Bank estimates of illiteracy in different parts of the world and also percentages of children at school. Once again, the figures can give only a general impression of educational deprivation. They tell us nothing about the type and quality of education – which, as we shall be arguing in a later section, are certainly as important as its volume.

1. Clifford, J., and Osmond, G., *World Development Handbook*, C. Knight for Overseas Development Institute, 1971.

8. Medical facilities, 1980	
Country	*Population per doctor*
USSR	270
USA	520
UK	650
Cuba	710
Japan	780
Egypt	970
Peru	1,390
South Korea	1,440
Colombia	1,710
Chile	1,930
Syria	2,270
Algeria	2,630
Brazil	2,810
Pakistan	3,480
India	3,690
Burma	4,660
Iran	6,090
Thailand	7,100
Ghana	7,630
Zambia	7,670
Kenya	7,890
Philippines	7,940
Indonesia	11,530
Ivory Coast	21,040

Source: ibid.

And finally, being poor means that you live a shorter life. Table 11 gives the life expectancy of the inhabitants of different parts of the world.

None of these indicators give a precise objective measure of poverty. But taken together they add up to a total picture of what it means to be poor. For the significant point is the extent to which they are related. Low incomes are closely associated with inadequate diet, poor health, sub-standard education and lower

9. Percentage of adult illiteracy for selected countries (latest available years)

Country	Total	Male	Female
USSR	0·2	n.a.	n.a.
USA	0·5	n.a.	n.a.
Spain	7·4	4·3	10·3
Philippines	17·4	15·7	19·1
Brazil	23·9	22·0	25·7
China	34·5	20·8	48·9
El Salvador	38·0	34·5	41·1
India	65·9	52·3	80·6
Nigeria	66·0	54·4	77·0
Ethiopia	95·8	91·7	99·8

Source: UNESCO Statistical Yearbook, 1984

10. Percentage of children enrolled in secondary school, 1981

USSR	96
Spain	88
UK	83
New Zealand	81
Malaysia	53
Egypt	52
Mexico	51
India	30
Nigeria	16
Guinea	16
Ethiopia	12

Note: secondary school age is generally considered to be 12–17.

Source: World Bank, op. cit.

life expectancy. That is because there are causal links between them summed up in the notion of a 'vicious circle of poverty'. Low productivity results in low income which leads to malnutrition, ill-health and insufficient education and therefore low productivity and low income.

| 11. Life expectancy at birth, 1982 | | |
Country	Male	Female
Japan	74	79
USA	71	78
UK	71	77
Chile	68	72
USSR	65	74
South Korea	64	71
Mexico	64	68
Philippines	62	66
Peru	57	60
Egypt	56	59
India	55	54
Burma	53	56
Pakistan	51	49

Source: ibid.

Much of the poverty which we have described in this section is *absolute* poverty – people living in conditions which should be intolerable by any standards. But poverty is also *relative*. What emerges from the figures is once again the extent to which the Rich and the Poor are worlds apart. One group enjoys standards of physical comfort and cultural opportunity quite inconceivable to the great majority.

The rest of this Part is concerned with other symptoms of underdevelopment. One is that poor countries are generally characterized by severe population pressure. Another is that born poor, your chances of finding adequate employment are abysmally low. But before dealing with these questions we look first at the divisions which exist *within* poor countries.

2. Development for whom?

Anyone who lived in a poor country in colonial times and who re-visits it today, a decade or two after independence, is bound to be struck by the evidence of economic change. Travelling in a superjet of the country's own international airline, he lands at an airport which, if he didn't know where he was, would offer him no clue to his whereabouts: for it is identical to those found on the outskirts of a dozen European capitals. He is whisked away in a Mercedes taxi along a modern highway to the city itself – with well-laid-out broad-pavemented streets bordered by fine large shops lavishly stocked with all the engaging gadgetry of modern society. In his air-conditioned hotel he sips iced Bourbon and dines from an international menu. The following morning he is collected by official car and shown the economic sights. He visits the new oil refinery, the industrial estate with a variety of modern consumer goods being produced by the most sophisticated of western techniques, the university – which differs from its counterparts at home only in the greater splendour of its architecture ... Yes, he agrees, this is development. Everywhere, the economic landscape is being transformed. The guide feeds him with statistics of road-building, bridges, power stations, ports.

And yet if he strays from the regular official route he will find himself in a very different environment, one which will be more familiar to that which he recalls from thirty years ago. For a start, the industrial estate is bounded by high meshed electrified fencing – to protect it from looting vandals in the shanty town of urban hopefuls which has sprung up on the perimeter of the city. And ten or twenty miles into the interior the villages through which he passes have hardly changed for a thousand years. The peasants continue to till the soil by gruelling traditional techniques. The motor car gives way to the bull-cart. Ragged children play in the dust (why are they not at school?). Little shops are sparsely stocked with sacks of grain, kerosene, sticky sweets festooned with flies ...

This is the phenomenon known as 'dualism' – the existence of a modern sector grafted on to a traditional society and separated from it by a gulf as wide as that which divides the world as a whole into Rich and Poor. Dualism is technological. The modern sector is mechanized, sometimes even automated, using the most up-to-date of capital-intensive techniques. The traditional sector continues to depend on primitive tools and handicraft methods of production. But dualism is also cultural. In the modern cities, the values and life-style are those of the west; only the rural areas serve to remind that this is a country with a quite different cultural background.

Economic change *has* taken place in most poor countries during the postwar period but all too frequently its incidence has been narrow, with the benefits accruing to only very limited sections of the population. One of the major charges which used to be levelled against colonialist powers was that when they did develop their colonial territories it was on an enclave basis – metropolitan islands of modernity in a surrounding sea of traditional poverty. Unfortunately, such distorted development has not disappeared with political independence. Inequalities within underdeveloped countries continue to be extreme and in very many cases are actually widening.

Most poor countries pay lip-service to egalitarian ideals. Notions of equality of status and opportunity, of classlessness and other socialist goals, are commonly written into constitutions and development plans. The declared intentions of most underdeveloped countries today reveal a conception of social justice markedly absent in the economic history of the earlier developers.

But, as with so many aspects of the development situation, between the conception and the execution falls the shadow of reality. Underdeveloped countries tend to be characterized by even greater concentrations of income and wealth than exist in the rich countries. The very rich class in poor economies are generally as rich or richer than their counterparts in developed economies. The poor are unimaginably poorer. Looking at fairly broad income strata, Griffin and Enos estimated that 'the inequalities are relatively, perhaps even absolutely, greater in the poor countries than in the rich. In the developed countries, the upper 10 per cent of the income earners typically receive about 30 per cent of the total pre-tax income; in the underdeveloped countries the upper 10 per cent typically receive over 40 per cent.'[2] Moreover, within these broad groups, there may be even more staggering concentrations of income. In Nicaragua in 1977, for example, the top 5 per cent of the population obtained no less than 28 per cent of the national income.[3]

2. Griffin, K. B., and Enos, J. L., *Planning Development*, Addison-Wesley, 1970, pp. 37–8.

3. Weber, H., *Nicaragua – the Sandinist Revolution*, Verso, 1981, p. 27.

Since it is also typically the case that in poor countries the opportunities for tax evasion are far wider than in developed countries, the distribution of *post-tax* incomes is likely to be still more uneven than in rich economies. And extreme inequality of income distribution reflects an even more disparate distribution of personal *wealth*.

Available evidence also suggests too that these inequalities are widening still further. Many years ago, Thomas Balogh warned that what was happening amounted to 'Polarization ... not only between the rich and the poor but between the poor themselves'.[4] He cited as an example the fact that employees in the 'modern' sector, such as bauxite workers in Jamaica, could earn 64 times as much as traditional rural workers in that country. More recently in the rural areas of Bangladesh the top 5 per cent of households saw their real income increase by 24 per cent between 1963–4 and 1976–7. The bottom 85 per cent of households saw their income decline by 33 per cent.[5]

Disparities in income and wealth are reflected in many other indicators, but generally the great divide is between the situation in a handful of urban complexes and of the vast majority of the population who continue to live in the rural areas. Educational opportunities and access to medical facilities, for example, are typically confined to urban dwellers, and particularly those in the higher income brackets. Such amenities, as we shall see, have often become vehicles for reinforcing rather than reducing privilege.

In recent years, yet another dimension of inequality has been added. This time it is *within* the poor rural sector itself. Primarily it is the result of the so-called 'green revolution'. New seed varieties of maize, wheat and rice developed in Mexico and the Philippines have made possible dramatically increased agricultural yields. But the opportunity of exploiting these new strains has been largely restricted to the already richer farmers. They require substantial inputs of fertilizers and pesticides and depend on abundant water being available. The number of farmers with this necessary capital and resources to make the new seed-types effective has proved to be very limited. Thus what has been heralded as a breakthrough

4. Balogh, T., House of Commons Select Committee on Overseas Aid, Minutes of Evidence, 1968–69, 1969–70, HMSO, p. 171.

5. Hartmann, B., and Boyce, J., *A Quiet Violence*, Zed, 1983, p. 270.

to agricultural revolution – however much it is to be welcomed as a means of increasing food supplies – has had the side-effect of leaving the mass of peasant farmers still further relatively impoverished.

Finally, inequality frequently takes a *regional* form. This is also a problem for rich countries. In Britain, for example, economic prosperity has been increasingly concentrated in the south-east and the area adjacent to London, with the rest of the country having lower earnings and higher unemployment. However, for most of the postwar period these imbalances have been the subject of official concern – with steps being taken, admittedly with only limited success, to minimize them. Underdeveloped countries, on the other hand, have not generally been active in promoting regional balance. In the tragic case of Pakistan, for example, development planning served to widen, rather than narrow, the gap between what was once the west of the country and the poorer east, now the separate nation of Bangladesh. Although they had roughly equal populations, the foreign exchange earned by eastern jute mainly financed industrialization in the west – and it was there, too, that the 'green revolution' mostly took place. The tensions and frustrations built up by such grotesquely lopsided development led to civil war and the creation of the independent state of Bangladesh in 1971.

Inequalities in poor countries thus take many forms. But nearly everywhere they are gross, and nearly everywhere they are increasing. Their existence is wildly at odds with the pious declarations of the governments of such countries. Their proclaimed objective is to reduce inequality, but the policies they pursue open still wider the chasm between rich and poor. Either this indicates such inadequacies in the planning machinery that governments are unable to control even the direction of economic and social change, let alone its degree, or it raises the suspicion that the egalitarian ideals which are expressed are no more than paper sentiments, electoral slogans which governing elites have no real intention of translating into practice.

Whether, besides this lamentable gap between promise and fulfilment, growing inequality within developing countries is a matter of concern depends on how the development mechanism is viewed. One school of economists, in the western tradition, sees widening disparities as the price to be paid for accelerating development, as its inevitable concomitant. For them, capital accumulation is the key to growth: they stress the importance of raising the rate of savings in underdeveloped economies to provide for a capital build-up, and they see in an unequal income distribution the best way of achieving it.

However, it can be questioned, firstly, whether a highly unequal income distribution *does* lead to higher savings in prevailing conditions. Or is it more likely to encourage 'conspicuous consumption' emulative of the standards of richer economies, as demonstrated by expatriates living in underdeveloped countries? But this is anyway not the heart of the matter. The crucial issue is whether it *is* lack of savings which forms the principal bottleneck to economic development – or whether it is human factors which are the more significant. Even if greater inequality *does* allow faster accumulation of physical capital, its effects might be offset by a further erosion of *human* capital. The World Health Organization has stressed that 'any social and economic development programme is primarily based on the availability and the potentialities of the human capital which is needed for developing the various sectors of a country's economy, its industry and its agriculture. Productivity depends to a considerable extent on the health and well-being of the labour force, because in order to mobilize human resources, there must exist the precondition that they are physically fit to be mobilized. Ill-health, under-nourishment, poor environmental conditions and debility affects the development process.'[6]

When inequalities are such that the living standards of the great mass of people are depressed to their present levels, development prospects look gloomy. In a situation where so many of the population of underdeveloped countries are suffering from malnutrition, improvements in diet, health and environmental conditions must be seen not as frittering away output in unnecessary consumption, but rather as a vital investment in human capital as a prerequisite of general development. There is now a growing body of economists who argue that greater equality is not merely a proper end of economic development but of crucial *instrumental* value in achieving it. Far from there being a conflict between

6. W H O I, para. doc AS/Ec/TR (22) 6.

economic development and social justice, they insist, with Myrdal, that 'inequality and the trend towards rising inequality stand as a complex of inhibitions and obstacles to development and that ... there is an urgent need for ... creating greater equality as a condition for speeding up development'.[7]

3. Too many mouths

One of the great difficulties of poor countries today is that in their development efforts they are aiming at a moving target. Nearly as fast as solutions are found to it, the development problem itself grows more acute. The main reason for this is the massive population pressure to which practically all underdeveloped countries are now subject. During the postwar period, the Poor World has been swept by a population explosion which has meant that substantial increases in output have been needed just to *maintain* existing income levels per head. Standing still has sometimes been an achievement in itself.

World population has already increased fivefold during the last two centuries; and on present trends will nearly double again by the year 2050. Even more to the point are the profoundly significant changes taking place in its distribution. Three quarters of the total are now inhabitants of less developed countries. But since poor countries have a population growth (averaging 2 per cent per annum) more than double that of the rich, it is a proportion which is going to greatly increase in coming decades. More and more people will be concentrated in those parts of the world least capable of providing for them.

Setting aside the relatively minor effects of migration, population growth depends on the balance between births and deaths. What lies behind the present population explosion is not a marked rise in fertility, but a spectacular fall in the death rate. Biologically, it seems that the maximum number of births which can take place each year per thousand people is about forty. Therefore in those long stretches of world history when world population remained static, we can assume that death rates must also have approximated

7. Myrdal, G., *The Challenge of World Poverty*, Allen Lane The Penguin Press, 1970, p. 50.

to that figure (4 per cent per annum). Professor Arthur Lewis's schematic stage analysis of falling death rates illustrates the nature of the population outburst.[8] For a start, ten deaths per thousand can be saved when food supplies improve – both because of increased production and because the danger of famine is reduced by better distribution; at this stage, if birth rates remain at 4 per cent, population will be increasing at 1 per cent. Another 1 per cent may be lopped off death rates by a 'public health revolution' – the eradication of endemic diseases like smallpox, malaria and the plague. And finally, death rates can be reduced to 1 per cent by the extension of individual medical care, with an adequate number of doctors, hospitals and clinics. At this last stage, population can expand at something like its biological maximum of 3 per cent per annum. ('Only' 3 per cent – but that is enough to double a population every twenty-five years.)

In present rich countries death rates have fallen to very low levels; but birth rates, too, after a time lag, have also dropped. In poor countries, birth rates have remained high – while at the same time dramatic cuts in the death rate have been achieved. And since there is still plenty of scope for further reductions in the death rate, it is quite possible for population to increase still faster than its present rate.

What, above all, has been responsible for reducing mortality rates in underdeveloped countries, has been the transfer of medical technology. For example, there was the famous Sri Lankan case, where anti-malarial spraying more than halved the death rate in the first postwar decade. Similar experience elsewhere led Michael Lipton once to describe the consequent population bulge of the 1970s as the 'DDT generation'. It is ironic that of all the attempts to diffuse development know-how to poor countries, it is the transfer of medical knowledge which has been most successful – and *that* has tended to add to rather than alleviate their problem. Why is it that a saving in deaths has been so much easier to achieve than an improvement in the means of supporting those whose lives have been saved? The answer lies partly in the cheapness of the new medical techniques: for instance, in the Sri Lankan case, the fall in

8. Lewis, W. A., *The Theory of Economic Growth*, Allen & Unwin, 1955, pp. 306–7.

death rates was the result of public health expenditures of only two dollars per head. But that is not the basic point. To increase *output* involves raising agricultural and industrial productivity – and that, as we shall see, can be accomplished only by a fundamental transformation of attitudes and institutions. No such transformation is needed for a public health revolution. A village can be sprayed against malaria without any change in customary outlook or traditional practice – without, indeed, any villager being aware of what is happening. Death control can be accomplished autonomously, without anything else changing. And that is where the problem lies. The present developed countries also experienced population explosions, but in their case economic growth had already taken firm hold so that output was rising faster than numbers. For poor countries, the demographic revolution has preceded their agricultural and industrial breakthroughs. For early developers, population increase was in many ways a factor stimulating further economic expansion – through widening markets, increasing the mobility of labour and a greater inducement to invest in new capital. But in the case of poor countries now, more people represents a major obstacle to continued development.

This is because, first of all, the age structure changes in a rapidly rising population. There are more mouths to feed – but not, at least for some time, more hands to work. Since it is infant mortality rates which are the most affected by public health measures, poor countries have a particularly high proportion of young people. This ratio of non-workers to workers is what demographers call the 'burden of dependency'. Those below the age of fifteen commonly comprise nearly half of the total population in developing countries. They contribute little or nothing to national production, but make heavy calls on the community's limited resources. They not only have to be fed and clothed, they must also be educated and trained – with a consequent diversion of investment resources from their alternative deployment in building new factories, fertilizer plants and other forms of physical capital. And a high burden of dependency, while *demanding* a higher level of investment, may, through depressing savings, reduce an economy's *capacity* to provide it.

Moreover, the problem is not just a short-term one which will be solved as the young people become active producers. On the one hand, as the bulge moves up, they also become active parents –

so that the rate of population increase gathers momentum still further. And on the other hand, although they now become potential members of the workforce, that will only mean more output if there are jobs for them to do. As we shall see in the next chapter, this is becoming an overwhelming task for most poor countries: to create enough jobs to absorb the increases in the labour force caused by the population explosion.

The Malthusian bogey, triumphantly overcome during the last century, may be abroad again with a vengeance. Many economists now see poor countries as caught in a 'low-level equilibrium trap' from which there is no obvious escape. Others, unwilling to be labelled as practitioners of a 'dismal science', argue that the pressure of population on resources creates a challenge which will force developing countries to a productive response: the bias of western optimism is shown in the assumption that challenges *are* always met. Others again suggest that simple projection of present trends is scaremongering. *One* of the reasons for present large families is that it used to be necessary to have, say, eight or ten children to guarantee one surviving male heir. Infant mortality has now been greatly reduced, but parents have not yet adjusted their family size to the new situation. When they do so, the rise in population will be damped down. But we know relatively little about the likely time lags involved between falling death rates and a subsequent fall in birth rates. And meanwhile there is the massive population increase already in the pipeline to be fed, educated and employed.

A growing consensus *has* emerged, however, about the need in poor countries for more extensive and determined population control policies. This means *birth* control measures, since there can be no question of easing the attack on what still remain by western standards quite high death rates. Studies suggest that the economic worth of preventing a birth in many low income countries may be up to two and a half times the annual per capita income. The cost of doing so, moreover, can now be kept at a very low level because of the availability of technical means – the pill, the loop, vasectomy – produced by modern technology. On this basis, the economic return to investment in birth control can be shown to be many times greater than that of output-increasing investment. That may be the theory. But what of the practice?

In fact, family planning was largely neglected in early development strategies. India was one of the first countries to undertake a programme aimed at reducing fertility, with its First Five Year Plan in 1951 stressing that 'The rapid increase in population and the consequent pressure on the limited resources available have brought to the forefront the urgency of problems of family planning. The main appeal for family planning is, however, based on considerations of the health and welfare of the family.'[9] But despite the urgency, the amount set aside for birth control measures amounted to a derisory 0·031 per cent of total planned spending – and only a sixth of that was actually spent. The mounting awareness of the importance of population control was shown in the way in which the Third Plan envisaged 'stabilizing the growth of population ... (as) ... at the very centre of planning development';[10] and in the Fourth Plan family planning was elevated to 'a programme of the highest importance',[11] taking over 2 per cent of total plan outlays and with specific targets for reduction in fertility rates being set.

Interest in curbing population growth has spread over the years to the point where today some three quarters of developing countries now have governmental population units aimed at reducing the fertility rates. The scale and nature of the programmes that have been implemented have varied widely – but there is no doubt that they have achieved substantial, if patchy, success. The 1984 *World Population Report* indicates that over the period 1970–75 to 1980–85 the average number of children born to a woman in developing countries declined by 26 per cent, from 5·5 to 4·1 children, but much of this overall figure is accounted for by the particularly successful Chinese programme, while in other parts of the world, notably Africa, no reduction has been experienced. The patchiness of success in this field partly lies in the real difficulties of *implementing* population policies – even when the will to do so is there.

There are three basic requirements for a successful family planning programme. The first is availability of cheap and acceptable contraceptive techniques. Second, there has to be an effective machinery to carry out the programme – of personnel, institutions

9. Delhi: Ministry of Information and Broadcasting, *First Five Year Plan*, 1953.
10. id., *Third Five Year Plan*, 1961.
11. id., *Fourth Five Year Plan Drafts*, 1969.

and propaganda. And thirdly, potential parents must be both
knowledgeable about the possibility of restricting their family size
and have the motivation to do so. Frequently these prerequisites
have been lacking in underdeveloped countries.

Medical technology has certainly created a variety of ways in
which births may be prevented. However, most of them have been
accompanied by unfortunate social or physical side effects, some
of which are only now being recognized – and it must be remembered that 'failures' in the context of a traditional society are likely
to be a good deal more damaging to confidence in a particular
contraceptive method than they are in an advanced economy. Then
again, inculcation of the idea and possibility of family planning
requires considerable numbers of paramedical staff who ideally
would have a remarkable combination of qualities: training, sympathy, diplomacy and willingness to work in the rural areas. But
this is precisely the type of personnel which is in short supply in
underdeveloped countries. There are few doctors and few nurses –
and those that there are find it far more profitable to practise
privately for the urban rich than to become birth control mission-
aries in the villages.

Above all, there is the question of motivation on the part of
potential parents. For one thing, birth control may be resisted on
religious grounds. But this, except in certain Catholic countries,
does not seem to have been a major problem. Much more serious
is the fact that in poor countries it may *pay* low income peasants
to have a large family, quite apart from the pleasure and social
kudos they may derive from doing so. After all, the private costs
of bringing up children may be quite small if State schooling is
provided freely. Against this, children may at quite a young age
begin to contribute to the family income by taking small jobs. Later
they provide the labour force for the family farm and they may
bring in marriage dowries. And most important of all, in an
extended family system, they are the guarantee of security in old
age for the parents. Large families in a poor society are thus a
substitute for a social security system. The peasants who persist in
producing large numbers of children may be acting with perfect
economic rationality from their individual viewpoints. It is no good
telling *them* that large families are contrary to the *community*
interest. Only when the general economic and social environment

is markedly improved can this conflict between social and private interest be fully resolved.

Certainly, however vigorous and successful a family planning policy, it does nothing about the 'pipeline' problem. If *no* more babies are born there after today, poor countries will still – because of the births which have already taken place – face many more years of a high burden of dependency and the need to find jobs for a massively increasing workforce. Family planning can relieve the present pressures by saving immediate consumption; but beyond that it must be seen as an investment for the future.

Furthermore, although the theoretical studies may suggest that there is a higher net yield from birth-saving than from output-increasing investment, population policy is no substitute for measures aimed at increasing productivity. Saving births can increase per capita income by limiting the number of mouths between which the national cake has to be shared. But it does little in itself to bring about those basic structural changes which are the essence of development. It is *that* transformation which is necessary to accelerate the rate at which the cake itself is increasing.

It remains true that 'development is the best contraception'. Family planning none the less has an important contributory role to play as a complement to positive development policies. It is unfortunate that governments and international agencies were slow to begin with in realizing the extent to which population growth could fritter away the benefits of development. But population pressure is *mainly* a symptom rather than a cause of underdevelopment; and it is on their success in dealing with the underlying problems of agriculture, industry, education and trade that the prospects of poor countries must ultimately depend.

4. And too many hands

The poorest of the poor are the growing millions throughout the underdeveloped world who can find no way of adequately supporting themselves and their families. There are many without jobs, and far more in occupations where what they can produce is pitifully little. Worklessness or the lack of sufficient productive work are now the most basic symptoms of underdevelopment.

In 1980 the recorded rate for unemployment in low-income Latin

American countries and the Caribbean was 8·1 per cent; in Asia it was 4·5 per cent and in Africa and the Middle East 14·8 per cent. With the re-emergence of mass unemployment in many of the rich western economies, these are no longer startlingly high rates.

But the comparison is highly misleading. In the first place, the figures are the *official* estimates – and such statistics in underdeveloped countries are notoriously unreliable. Indeed, this is yet another symptom of underdevelopment. Even in Britain or similar countries with an efficient machinery for the collection of data and where there is incentive for people to register for welfare benefits to which they are entitled, there is still fierce controversy about just how many there are unemployed. Identifying the number out of work in a poor country which lacks the facilities to collect accurate statistics, where there are few, if any, job centres and no social security benefits, is a far more difficult task.

Second, and more important, is the fact that such 'unemployment' figures anyway represent only the tip of the iceberg. Far more significant are the vast numbers who are more or less 'underemployed'. Many of these will be helping out on the family smallholding, perhaps with some seasonal wage-earning from working for a better-off landholder. Or they may secure a place in an already overstaffed office or in a private household as a domestic servant. And then there are the self-employed – the shoe cleaners, the bicycle tyre pumpers, the barbers, the match sellers, who line the streets of any poor town, engaged in petty trading. What they all have in common is that they add little or perhaps nothing to the total volume of output. The social structure provides its own system of work-*sharing* to compensate for the lack of new productive job opportunities. But it also generally implies the sharing of already appallingly low incomes. In 1977 the ILO estimated that no less than 35 per cent of the entire labour force in the Third World was underemployed.

In many rich western countries today, again facing unemployment problems that it once seemed had been conquered, there is a bitter debate between Keynesian and monetarist economists about what should be done. But neither set of policy prescriptions can have more than limited relevance in the case of present-day developing countries.

(i) Keynesians point to inadequate spending as the main cause of unemployment, i.e. demand-deficiency. For them, the answer lies in governments manipulating the overall level of spending to just that required to buy full employment output.

But if governments in poor countries were simply to pump in additional demand through tax cuts or by spending more than they received in taxation, what would happen? Much of the higher incomes would be spent on necessities, pushing up the price of food (if it was not regulated). In a rich market economy, higher prices are supposed to act as a signal to producers to expand output. But in a poor country, this may not happen. With traditional techniques, farmers may not find it possible to increase production; some may even see higher prices as an opportunity to supplement their own inadequate food consumption – so that marketed output actually falls. If there are supply 'inelasticities' of this kind, then pumping in purchasing power may certainly lead to inflation rather than growth of production – to find an outlet in expanded demand for imports, worsening the balance of payments.

The point is that unemployment in poor countries is generally of labour only. There is not a great degree of idle capital or other co-operant factors of production with which unemployed labour can be combined to yield increases in output in response to just demand stimulation.

(ii) Monetarist or 'classical' views about the causes and cures for unemployment seem even less appropriate to the problem confronting developing countries. Unemployment, it is said, is due to wages being too high. This results in a glut of labour on the market which will be cleared only by a fall in wages to a level at which employers will be prepared to hire those who are unemployed.

The logic of this theory is highly questionable, and evidence that wage cuts would stimulate employment, even in rich countries, is hard to come by. But in the case of poor countries with already low wage levels, it is quite possible that even if there were a theoretical 'equilibrium' wage rate at which the labour market would clear itself, this might prove to be below the subsistence level needed for the workforce physically to survive.

The nature of unemployment and underemployment in poor countries is complex. The background is the pressure of rapidly growing population which, as we have already seen, means vast numbers of fresh recruits each year to the army of those already seeking work. Millions of new jobs must be created for young people who have not yet joined the workforce, as well as dealing with the backlog of those at present underused. The World Bank has estimated that in 1975 the labour force in developing countries was about 750 million and by the turn of the century will be over 1,200 million.

And yet development planning has commonly been biased towards capital intensive, long gestation techniques of production. Particularly in the earlier years, investment projects too often embodied the most up-to-date technology – based on the very different western situation of labour shortage rather than abundance. It *can* be argued that this is the best long-run solution to the unemployment problem: heavy industries built up now will create *more* labour absorption at a later date. However, the immediate cost in terms of rising unemployment has been very high and the efficiency of the strategy is in any case questionable; given very limited capital resources, the number of jobs which can be created using capital-intensive techniques is derisory compared with the number needed. Moreover, an additional effect of grafting such a technology indiscriminately on to a traditional economy is the destruction of indigenous craft enterprises – adding to underutilization of labour through a form of technological unemployment.

Moreover, there has frequently been an emphasis on industrialization as the road to development, with a relative neglect of the rural sector. This has been coupled in many cases with an educational sense of values that attracts young people in particular to the excitement of the modern, if squalid, urban sector. To some extent, the lure of the towns stems from the substantially higher wage rates earned by those who *are* lucky enough to find industrial unemployment – earnings kept high by minimum wage legislation and union bargaining strength which have created new urban elites. There may be more glamour and hope in seeking work in the towns than in drifting underemployed in the traditional village. However, the urban industries cannot provide the necessary number of jobs.

The case of Kenya, examined in the World Bank's *World Development Report 1984*, illustrates the scale of the problem. Only about 14 per cent of the Kenyan labour force is in wage employment in the 'modern' sector. Between 1972 and 1980 that modern sector grew by a highly successful 4·3 per cent a year (faster than Japan at the end of the nineteenth century), while the labour force grew by 3·5 per cent each year. Non-wage employment, mainly in agriculture, absorbed over 80 per cent of the increase in labour. Even if the population grows more slowly in future, the rural sector will still have to absorb over 70 per cent of the growth in workers for the rest of the century. In 1976 there were 1·2 million Kenyans employed in the modern sector and 3·8 million in agriculture. By the year 2000 the modern sector will have to find a further 1·8 million jobs and the land provide for an extra 6·6 million, if unemployment is not to increase.

These are all matters to which we shall return shortly. But at this stage it is worth re-emphasizing the difficulties of comparing the employment problems of rich and poor countries. 'Unemployment' and 'underemployment' are western terms which it is dangerous to apply too glibly to underdeveloped countries. They carry with them inapplicable implications of 'full employment' norms. In developed economies, it is not unreasonable to calculate the 'loss' of output caused by unemployment – on the assumption that the unemployed, if working, would do so for a conventional working week, at a given intensity and with a given productivity in line with the national average. But none of these assumptions can be validly carried over to poor countries, where the problem of development is essentially one of how to *change* these variables. Questions of how to provide productive opportunities for the growing labour force, of changing attitudes, institutions and strategies to make this possible – these lie at the very heart of the development problem.

PART THREE
INSIDE THE POOR WORLD

1. What are they trying to do?

How should we measure the progress of developing countries in their striving for development? What indeed *is* economic development? Since the outstanding feature of underdeveloped countries is their economic poverty it seems reasonable to look, first of all, at how much richer they are becoming year by year. Information on this question is produced by national income statisticians who aggregate the value of all goods and services produced annually by an economy into a total known as gross domestic product (GDP). Changes in the total from one year to the next (after allowing for the effects of general price movements) represent the rate of economic growth in the economy.

On this criterion, the postwar record of the underdeveloped countries has been quite impressive. As a group they achieved a growth rate of no less than 6·3 per cent per annum between 1960 and 1973 – a dramatic acceleration from what had been managed in the early decades of the century. For 1973–9, after the Organization of Petroleum Exporting Countries' (OPEC) dramatic increase in oil prices, 5·2 per cent was averaged (although by the early

1980s the world recession had resulted in average growth rates in developing countries plunging to a mere 1 per cent). Admittedly, this average figure conceals wide variations in continental and national performances; but underdeveloped countries as a whole managed during most of the 1970s to grow almost twice as fast as the industrialized economies, which averaged a 2·8 per cent growth rate. And when compared with the historical record of some of the early developers the recent performance of present underdeveloped countries looks even more spectacular. Britain, it will be remembered, with all its advantages of being first in the field, managed far less rapid growth rates during the nineteenth century.

However, although it still remains common practice, it is highly questionable whether it is legitimate to use national income statistics in this way and to equate economic growth with economic development.

12. Annual average rate of growth of GDP 1973–9 (per cent)	
Underdeveloped countries	5·2
Low income	4·8
Asia	5·2
Africa	2·1
Middle income, oil importers	5·6
Middle income, oil exporters	4·9
Industrial market economies	2·8

Source: World Bank, World Development Report 1984, OUP, 1984

For one thing, the gross domestic product figures tell us nothing about the degree of population pressure. For this, national output has to be reduced to per capita terms. A growth rate of 3 per cent in GDP means, of course, only a constant output per head if population has meanwhile grown at the same rate: the increased output has all been eaten up in providing for the increased numbers. And although even standing still may represent a considerable achievement in face of rapid population growth (particularly since it will be concentrated initially in non-working age groups), growth per capita in underdeveloped countries compares unfavourably with that achieved by industrialized economies.

Then again, the distinction between gross *domestic* product and gross *national* product is an important one for many developing countries. Domestic product is the output of the economy as a whole regardless of whether it is produced by nationals or foreigners. National product is the total which remains after payments of profits and interest to foreign owners of capital have been deducted. For many poor countries the difference between the two is very substantial indeed – with the degree to which the fruits of growth are accruing to foreigners being obscured by concentration on the domestic product figures.

13. Average annual rate of growth per capita, 1973–9 (per cent)	
Underdeveloped countries	2·0
Low income	2·9
Asia	3·3
Africa	−1·0
Middle income	3·3
Major exporters of manufactures (newly industrialized countries)	3·6
Oil exporters	2·3
Industrial market economies	2·1

Source: ibid.

Technical problems loom very large in interpreting national income statistics from poor countries. National income accounting is still a very recent technique. Even in developed countries its widespread application dates back only to the last war. But in rich western countries we are now fairly good at it. The population is sufficiently educated and the administrative network sufficiently widely cast and efficient for a vast amount of information to be made available to government departments. Every year an enormous range and depth of data is accumulated on production, population, exports and imports, incomes and so on. And the statistical expertise is there, not only to collect such facts, but also then to collate them into useful and meaningful patterns. Even so, there are a number of headaches for national income accountants. When I grow vegetables in my back garden I contribute towards national output; strictly, this ought to appear in the accounts – but in practice it is left out because production of this kind is only a negligible proportion of the total. Problems also arise with output which is not marketed – like social services or the flow of satisfaction derived from house ownership; here, the national income statisticians either have to value at the cost of production or 'impute' a value. In collecting information on so vast a scale, errors and omissions are bound to occur; sometimes it is genuinely doubtful whether output last year grew by, say, 1·5 per cent or declined by 0·5 per cent.

All of these are purely technical problems of calculating national income data which exist even in rich countries. They make detailed comparisons of national income over time subject to a significant margin of error. When it comes to *interpreting* the results we move into a far more controversial area. We have become used in Britain and other developed countries to regarding growth of national output as the index of 'progress'. Politicians in the postwar period have frequently expressed their view of national progress in terms of faster growth. But writers like Mishan[1] and Galbraith[2] have stressed that economic growth is only a means rather than an end of policy and may even *impede* the achievement of important social goals. The index very often serves to conceal more than it reveals. Three questions always need to be asked about any given rate of economic growth. First, growth of what? Guns or butter? Hospitals or electric toothbrushes? Public or private goods? We should be as vitally interested in the *composition* of output as in its total. Second, who has benefited from growth? How has income *distribution* been affected? An increase in income per capita may hide the fact that a few have become better off and the majority worse off. Once again, this is the sort of question about which we are all much concerned. And third, what have been the *costs* of growth? Has increased production been achieved only at the expense of less leisure, a more hectic pace of life, social upheaval or loss of amenity? And if so, was it worth it?

One final limitation of the growth index is worth stressing. Economists sometimes like to pretend that figures for national economic growth are objective, scientific measurements, quite

1. Mishan, E. J., *The Costs of Economic Growth*, Staples Press, 1967; Penguin Books, 1969.
2. Galbraith, J. K., *The Affluent Society*, Hamish Hamilton, 2nd edn, 1969; Penguin Books, 1970.

distinct from political questions of income distribution which involve the use of 'value judgements'. In fact, they are nothing of the sort. In drawing up the aggregate figures, output is valued at its current market prices, prices which are determined by the supply and demand for the various goods and services. But what, in turn, determines the relative strengths of demand? As much as anything else, it is the *prevailing income distribution*. If tomorrow it was decreed that incomes in this country should be immediately equalized, then the prices of nearly everything would be bound to change – as the demand for some goods rose and for some fell. If at this stage national output was re-calculated, a quite different total value would emerge. In other words, output totals are a *reflection* of the underlying income distribution. It is impossible to separate questions of 'efficiency' from value-loaded considerations of equitable distribution.

These problems which arise in calculating and interpreting national income statistics in rich countries become far more acute when the technique is transplanted to the quite different situation of poor countries. At every stage the difficulties are compounded. They begin at the grassroots level of collection of data. With widespread illiteracy and poverty, a large part of the population is outside the official network. The consequent need for rough sampling, and the weakness and corruptibility of local administration, means that the information fed back to the centre is highly unreliable. Moreover, a substantial part of the output in underdeveloped countries is not sold on the open market at all but is self-consumed by subsistence farmers. This creates enormous problems in determining what value should be imputed for such output. Peasants questioned about how much they produce are deeply suspicious of the uses to which such information might be put and they may lie accordingly. Basic data like that of population censuses may be manipulated according to the ruling party's political interest. The official statistics, even given an administration genuinely concerned to provide accurate information, is subject to such margins of error that a statement from a politician in an underdeveloped country that 'last year our national income rose by 2·9 per cent' can be regarded as no more than an exercise in optimistic sophistry. Most of the preconditions for accurate national income accounting are missing in a poor country; and their absence is in itself a symptom of under-development.

And if the growth figures *were* reliable, what should we make of them? Setting aside the technical problems, how legitimate is it to equate growth with *development*? There are, after all, a number of cases in which economic growth has taken place during the postwar years but to which the 'development' label could only very dubiously be attached. Take, for example, some of the oil states – like Kuwait or Saudi Arabia – which have experienced rapid rates of growth in output. Kuwait indeed has one of the highest per capita incomes in the world: but can it be described as a developed country? The affluence of all these countries has stemmed from the foreign exploitation of a single product – petroleum. Royalties are the source of their increased incomes – and they are very unequally distributed. But beyond this, how much has changed? If the oil were suddenly to dry up, how far would these countries be in a position to maintain their past growth rates? It is doubt about the extent to which they *have* brought about changes in the underlying economic and social structure which suggests that they have 'grown' a good deal more than they have 'developed'.

The other side of the coin is that economic development can be taking place which is not always reflected in immediate growth rates. Establishment of infrastructure – roads, schools, hospitals – can create a base for future material advance while yielding little in the way of increased output now. Merely maintaining existing per capita incomes may represent a development achievement – in face, for example, of enormous population pressures as in India or the flight of skilled personnel from post-revolutionary Cuba. The 'cultural revolution' in China was possibly part of the development process – but its immediate effects on the economy were highly disruptive.

So what, then, is there about economic *development* which distinguishes it from growth? In the first place, it is sometimes said that growth is a measurement only of quantitative change – while economic development involves *qualitative* transformation; moreover, the development label should be reserved for cases in which growth is being directed towards the achievement of such goals as full employment, equality and social justice. There are economists of this opinion, who argue that value considerations like these must be explicitly spelled out in the very definition of development. But this means that we can use the term 'development' to refer only to those societies which happen to conform with our own value premises. Perhaps this is rather too restrictive. For in practice, 'capitalist' commentators may want to describe a situation such as that of Communist China as one of development (although not the type that they would recommend); and similarly 'socialist' historians may well apply the term to, for example, nineteenth-century Britain – despite the fact that the mass of people possibly became temporarily worse off during the course of the industrial revolution.

There is no question of trying to keep economics 'value-free'. Perhaps most of all in the field of development, economics is quite inextricably mixed with political and social considerations. But there is something to be said none the less for defining development in a way which leaves it open for us to go on to say 'But it is a form of development of which I don't personally approve' or 'Economic development has taken place but it has been narrowly based; social development has lagged behind'.

Suppose that growth is defined as the result of increased economic efficiency *within* a given structure of socio-political attitudes and institutions. Then development can be distinguished as the process of *altering* that structure. The distinction is one which is applicable in rich as well as in poor countries. In Britain, for instance, the economy grows from year to year without any very basic changes being brought about. And when in Britain we talk about the possibility and desirability of increasing growth rates, what we may really be seeking is *development*; faster growth means eradicating dilettantism, the inculcation of more drive and dynamism, increased flexibility and mobility. Given basic changes of this kind (and their desirability is, of course, highly debatable) then a higher growth rate may emerge. Thus development is not entirely divorced from growth. There can be growth without corresponding development. But development, on the other hand, is unlikely – except in the short run – to occur without growth. Ultimately, unless the objectives of a society are explicitly non-material, economic development will tend to be reflected, although not always closely, in the rate of economic growth.

Development, therefore, means bringing about basic changes in the underlying social fabric of attitudes and institutions so that the objectives of the society can be more fully realized. And in this transformation, it is important that the mass of people are *involved*. They may not be immediate beneficiaries – the process of development has often proved to be a painful one; but unless the process is genuinely participatory, with a *general* awareness of change and of the need to adjust to it, then it is doubtful if it can be sustained. Successful long-term development requires a powerful motivating *ideology*. It may take a variety of forms – capitalist competition, nationalism, religious fervour, socialist emulation; but without some such underlying drive it is very difficult to maintain the development impetus.

On these criteria, the performance of poor countries during recent decades is a great deal less satisfactory than when they are judged by their record of economic growth. Some have hardly begun to face up to the need for basic reorientation which is implied in the development process. In many, the locus of change has been so limited as to be self-defeating. The nature of such failures and their causes are the subject of the following sections.

2. Planning for development

All underdeveloped countries *plan* for development. How far they do so, and what form it takes, varies widely: the spectrum ranges from China and Cuba at one extreme, to Thailand and the Philippines at the other. But they all plan. Planning, after all, simply means systematic intervention by the State to bring about changes which would not otherwise happen. Beyond that, it can mean most things to most people. It may be comprehensive – involving a broad *macro*-economic approach to affect the 'big' aggregate variables in the economy like national investment, the price level or the balance of payments; or it may be piecemeal – a series of exercises in *micro*-economic intervention, directed at particular areas of the economy and social system. Its purpose may be 'stimulatory', designed to identify or create the conditions in which the *private* sector can flourish; or it may be 'compensatory', with the State itself undertaking economic and social activities to make good the deficiencies of the private sector. It may be authoritarian or permissive – imposing a pattern from above or merely bringing together interested parties to reveal their common interest in solving development problems. In their objectives, scope and mechanisms, there is an infinite gradation of plans.

But whatever form it takes, all poor countries aiming at development undertake social and economic planning. They do so because development has *not* taken place *spontaneously*. Left to its own devices, the economic and social system has not delivered the goods. Commitment to development therefore implies a scheme of action, of whatever degree, to bring about changes which are either not taking place otherwise or are occurring too slowly.

The ideal market mechanism

British development, and that of most other earlier developers, *was* largely spontaneous, with the State intervening hardly at all. Behind this *laissez-faire* approach lay the whole weight of 'classical' economic thinking (which still occupies a surprising proportion of most economics textbooks). Adam Smith and his successors argued that economic progress was best secured by leaving individuals to get on with the job, unhampered by State interference. Pursuit of individual self-interest would, fortunately, simultaneously promote the maximum social good. The means through which this would be achieved, Adam Smith's 'invisible hand', was the price system or market mechanism.

The economic problem was seen as one of resource allocation. On the one hand we have resources – land, labour and capital – which are scarce and capable of many uses. And on the other hand, there are the consumers – with apparently unlimited wants. The problem, then, is how to get resources into just those lines of production which will maximize consumer satisfactions. The way to do it, said the classical economists, was the market mechanism. Consumers, seemingly remote from resources, were in fact indirectly in touch through the intermediary of *firms*.

The working of the ideal market mechanism is one of economic democracy. Consumers each have a certain number of 'votes' (their incomes) which they cast, according to their tastes, in the market for goods and services. These votes are then collected by the firms – how many each gets depending on whether their goods are popular or not. But that is not the end of the matter, because the market process is one of indirect democracy. The firm is only an

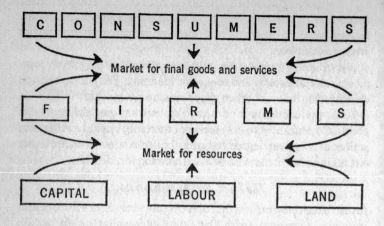

intermediary. The next stage is that the firm then re-casts the votes in the market for resources. And the amount of land, labour and capital which each firm can command is determined by the weight of its consumer votes. If consumer tastes switch to a particular good, they will cast more votes for it (i.e. bid up its price). This will enable the producer to command more resources than before – at the expense, of course, of other producers for whose goods demand has fallen off. Thus consumers, although they have no direct contact with resources, can through the price mechanism make their preferences clear and ensure that resources are channelled into just those lines of production which will maximize their satisfactions.

Does it work?

For the market mechanism to do its job properly, prices must reflect two things: consumer preferences and cost of production. And when the two are balanced against each other there is said to be an 'optimum' allocation of resources – in the sense that it is impossible to shift production from one line to another without making someone worse off than before. Over the years the price mechanism has come under heavy fire even in developed economies. It has been suggested that the conditions necessary for prices to act as accurate signals are unlikely to be met in modern industrial societies. Also seriously questioned is whether the so-called 'optimum', which would result if they did, is a significant or even acceptable state to aim for. Limitations of the market mechanism in practice have served as the rationale for major State involvement in the running of most developed economies.

The appropriateness of relying on the price mechanism in underdeveloped countries is even more questionable.

(i) For prices to serve as effective signposts for the direction of resources, markets must be relatively 'perfect'. That is, consumers must cast their votes rationally on the basis of full information; firms must pass on the votes they receive and be responsive to changing consumer demands; and resources must be mobile enough to be shifted from one type of production to another. In fact, markets in underdeveloped economies tend to be highly imperfect. Consumers may be ignorant of the options open to them and fragmented into unconnected markets by poor communications. Firms can pocket consumer votes for themselves (as monopoly profits) rather than pass them on as demand for resources; resources are typically even more immobile than they are in rich countries. Prices, instead of delicately reflecting the relative strengths of demand and supply, are profoundly distorted by underlying market imperfections.

(ii) In a pure market system, consumers and producers both work to maximize their own individual gains. All that are taken into account in the price calculus are *private* costs and benefits. But the operations of a firm may create costs for the rest of the community which do not show up in its own balance sheet, e.g. increased urban congestion or river pollution. Similarly, a loss-making project from the point of view of one firm may yield net economic benefits to society as a whole. Significant divergence between private and social costs and benefits are particularly likely in less developed economies because investment decisions there tend to be more risky and to depend for their success on others making complementary investments elsewhere in the economy.

(iii) And how relevant anyway is the 'optimum' itself – that allocation of resources which would 'ideally' result from the working of an unimpeded market mechanism? It is an optimum *only* in the sense that nobody can be made better off without making someone worse off. In other words, it corresponds to the existing income distribution, and, as we pointed out in discussing the meaning of development, prices are a reflection of that distribution. In the typical conditions of underdeveloped countries where income inequalities are extreme – and in which, therefore, consumers have wildly varying numbers of 'votes' – just how acceptable therefore is a pattern of production which results from the price mechanism?

(iv) Moreover, the price system is essentially concerned with *allocative* efficiency. As we have learned in developed countries in practice the market does not guarantee that resources will all be fully employed: that is because millions of individual consumption and production decisions are very likely to add up to the wrong *total*. Even less is it geared to *expanding* the productive possibilities of an economy. But that *is* the question that we are concerned with in development economics. The development task is not so much one of bringing about marginal changes in the production pattern within a given framework of institutions and attitudes as of altering that framework itself – to yield more capital accumulation, higher labour productivity and greater entrepreneurial drive. It is to do with the process of dynamic change, rather than the static efficiency gains of the market mechanism model. In promoting development it is often better, as Kenneth Boulding once put it, 'to be half way up a mountain than at the top of a molehill'.

It is because of these deficiencies of the market mechanism that governments in developed countries have intervened more actively in their economies in the postwar period than ever before. For poor countries – with their greater market imperfections, wider divergencies of social and private costs and benefits, and their need to regard income redistribution and structural transformation as essential elements of change – the need to plan is even greater.

However, this is not to eulogize planning. Planning is no panacea. The setting out of appropriate objectives does not guarantee their fulfilment. Planning is only a step forward when it succeeds in *overcoming* the defects of the market system. Sometimes it has been over-ambitious and misdirected, centred on western concepts of dubious applicability, and requiring resources and techniques which poor countries lack. Sometimes planning itself has distorted and stifled the development effort.

The appropriate scope and nature of planning depends on the particular circumstances of the underdeveloped country concerned. Griffin and Enos in their *Planning Development* distinguish between two broad approaches. One is that of the 'model builders, general programmers and simulators ... concerned with collecting data, econometric estimation and the construction of a consistent model of the economy'. This is a comprehensive form of planning on the assumption that 'the institutional environment is a constant'. The other is 'an exercise in removing bottlenecks ... more interested in isolating, analysing and solving specific problems ... (and) ... frequently assumes that institutions are variables'.[3]

The first of these approaches may often be over-demanding of administrative skills and data-availability for most underdeveloped countries: development consultants advising underdeveloped countries are all too prone to suggest planning mechanisms far more ambitious than those which have already been tried in the basically more favourable circumstances of developed economies. And success in the second approach depends heavily on the existence of the necessary political will to overcome often deeply entrenched resistance to change.

Whatever form it takes, the purpose of planning is to move towards a set of objectives according to a pre-conceived strategy. It is to the nature of these objectives and strategy that we now turn.

3. Some awkward choices

The selection of a development strategy for a poor country is commonly presented in terms of a series of agonizing choices. The three discussed here are all variants of the same theme – that development involves a tightening of belts today in order to have Jam Tomorrow.

The first of these choices is that between a capital build-up for the future and consumption now. One of the main symptoms of underdevelopment is that a poor country lacks the massive stock of capital – factories, machines, schools, hospitals, houses, roads, bridges, railways, ports – which the rich countries have steadily accumulated over the years. The success of poor countries in increasing production therefore depends, it is argued, on their ability to make good this capital shortage. But using resources to

3. Griffin, K. B., and Enos, J. L., *Planning Development*, Addison-Wesley, 1970, pp. 28–9.

build factories and machines means that they *can't* be used for present consumption. However, sacrifices today will bring rewards tomorrow. Three broad strategic alternatives offer themselves.

(i) *Heavy* strategy. This approach involves the maximum sacrifice of present consumption. Any surplus production over immediate requirements is used to create a complex of 'basic' industries similar to that which exists in developed countries. This is a strategy which exploits a peculiarity of such basic industries – their ability to reproduce themselves. It is, for instance, a steel mill strategy – with the output of the mill being used to create more steel mills. It is a strategy of plough-back – in which the consumption of present generations is deliberately held low for the benefit of posterity. Only when the structure of basic industries becomes that appropriate to a developed country will the output of the heavy industries finally be diverted into producing machines to produce consumer goods. It is a strategy similar to that pursued in the Soviet Union in the thirties.

(ii) *Consumption* strategy. Here the emphasis is on relieving immediate poverty through maximizing the *present* flow of consumer goods produced by traditional techniques. But, it is argued, since this leaves nothing for capital accumulation, any initial increase in living standards can at best only be maintained and may, in face of population pressure, even fall.

(iii) *Intermediate* strategy. This is a combination of the other two. There is an initial build-up of basic industries, but their output is then used to make machinery designed to increase the supply of consumer goods.

Corresponding to these three strategies are different time paths of development.

What this crude characterization of the choice of strategies highlights is the importance of *time* in development planning. It is not enough to say, for example, that the development objective is to maximize output. The question then arises of – output when? There is an obvious analogy with the individual. Suppose that I am offered £100 now or a sum of money in five years' time. Then in principle I can decide how much I am prepared to accept five years hence which will have the same value to me as the £100 today. In working out what it is, I shall be expressing my rate of *time preference*. Similar choices have to be made for society as a whole.

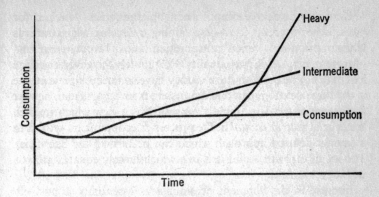

A second basic choice said to be facing development planners is that between maximizing output and maximizing employment. We have already seen that an enormous number of new jobs need to be created in underdeveloped countries in order to absorb the increases in their workforce caused by the population explosion. Here again, the development planner may feel confronted with a basic dilemma. An immediate alleviation of the unemployment problem may involve the use of traditional labour-intensive techniques of production – spreading the available amount of capital thinly between large numbers of workers. But, it is argued, such techniques are likely to lead to only a slow growth of output – and also, because they will result in a high wage–profit ratio, to relatively little plough-back. Maximizing growth, on the other hand, using modern capital-intensive techniques, aggravates the immediate unemployment problem, which becomes soluble only as the modern sector expands. A painful choice thus has to be made about the acceptable 'trade-off' between the two conflicting objectives.

And thirdly, the development dilemma is sometimes presented as involving a choice between the achievement of social or economic objectives. Socially, an underdeveloped country may aspire to a more egalitarian distribution of income and wealth. But, it is often argued, an unequal distribution provides the savings potential and incentives necessary for rapid growth. Policies directed at achieving the social objective will therefore be at the expense of the economic objective. This is an argument which we have already briefly examined in Part Two, Section 2.

Here, then, are three examples of agonizing choices which might have to be faced up to in determining a development strategy. Consumption now *versus* consumption later. Output *versus* employment. Growth *versus* equality. Fortunately, however, the choices may not be quite so stark as they have so far been presented.

All three development dilemmas stem from a particular view of the nature of the development process. It is a view which stresses the crucial role of *capital* in the process of economic growth. It is a savings-centred approach which can be termed the Sacrificial Theory of Growth – and it is one which largely equates growth with development.

Interest in development economics is essentially a postwar phenomenon, arising from the revelation of problems of underdevelopment which had been concealed by colonial independence. But coinciding with the emergence of a new political framework for poor countries was the fact that economists in rich countries, apparently having solved the problem of cyclical unemployment, could direct their attention to the ways in which growth rates in developed economies could be further stimulated. In looking at this problem, economists produced in the first instance a basically very simple model.

The growth of an economy, they argued, depended essentially on the rate at which it could accumulate capital which could be used to expand output in the future. Suppose that the economy has an output of £10,000 million per annum produced by a stock of capital of £30,000 million. The ratio of capital to output is thus 3:1. That is, it takes three units of capital to produce one unit of output. Now if the economy is to grow at 5 per cent per annum, i.e. expand output by £500 million, the increase in capital stock needed to achieve this is £1,500 million. But in order to invest this amount in new plant and machinery, equivalent resources have to be released from current consumption. In other words, to secure a 5 per cent growth rate, the community will have to save (not spend) some 15 per cent of its income, devoting it to a capital build-up which will yield future benefits. (This is the amount needed for *new* investment; in addition, further savings are necessary to *maintain* the existing capital stock.)

Growth economists during the immediate postwar period were primarily concerned with the problems of developed countries. But a similar analysis soon came to be applied to the underdeveloped economies. And here the problem was seen to be far more acute. This was firstly because population increase of 2·5–3 per cent per annum meant that increased per capita incomes required growth in excess of *that*. And secondly, initially very low incomes meant that the necessary levels of savings would be very difficult to secure.

14. Growth, population and savings	
% increase in population	*Alternative % per capita growth targets*
3	2
3	3
3	4

Required % growth of output	*Capital-output ratio*	*Required savings ratio*
5	3	15%
6	3	18%
7	3	21%

Thus a modest 2 per cent growth in per capita income would require that 15 per cent of current income was saved. 3 per cent growth would mean an 18 per cent savings ratio. And 4 per cent increase in income per head could be achieved only if 21 per cent of national income was set aside for capital accumulation. Since underdeveloped countries were poor, they were caught in a vicious circle. Low income meant low savings leading to little capital accumulation resulting in a slow rate of growth and low incomes.

However, the savings-centred theory is suspect both as an explanation of past growth and as the key to future development. It posits a dominant role for capital accumulation which is supported by neither historical nor comparative evidence. Although economic historians such as Walt Rostow have suggested that an essential element in the so-called 'take-off' period in which countries embark on modern growth is an increase in their productive investment 'from 5 per cent to, say, 10 per cent' of their national incomes, case studies of the earlier developers do not reveal any dramatic rise in savings to account for their material advance. Nor is the present correlation between growth rates and savings ratios in different countries a close one. And even if it were, might it not be the case that the *causal* relationship was the reverse of that postulated in the Sacrificial Theory of Growth – that it was faster growth which caused more rapid capital accumulation rather than the other way round?

Then again, in developed countries subsequent studies of growth rates, and of why they differ from economy to economy, suggest that capital is only one of many factors in the growth process. Technological change, industrial structure, education, planning, and alteration of social attitudes and institutions, all play important parts. What has become clear is that growth can seldom be secured by the manipulation of a single economic variable like the savings ratio. This is likely to be still truer of underdeveloped countries where the development problem is not so much one of squeezing more savings out of the economy on the assumption that the underlying conditons remain constant – but rather of altering the parameters of the system itself.

The whole conceptual basis of the Sacrificial Theory is of very dubious applicability to the situation of underdeveloped countries. It rests, in particular, on the assumption that a distinction *can* be clearly drawn between consumption and investment. Even in developed countries, the matter of quite where to draw the dividing line between them causes considerable headaches for the national income statisticians. If consumption is that part of output which gives current satisfaction and investment is that part set aside for the future, then how, for example, should we classify houses and other durable consumer goods which yield a stream of satisfaction over time?

The problems of using the same conceptual toolbox to analyse poor-country situations are infinitely more acute. 'When living and nutritional standards are low – as is typically the case for much of the population in underdeveloped societies – a higher volume of "consumption", combined with qualitative changes in its composition, is often a prerequisite of substantial improvments in labour efficiency and productivity. For this reason, it is quite conceivable that increases in "consumption" – rather than simply adding to the satisfactions of the consuming agent – might have a positive effect on future production and indeed may be indispensable to its achievement.'[4] Improved sanitation and hygiene, better health, and even 'incentive' consumer goods – may all have an important instrumental role in promoting development which cuts across the traditional consumption-investment distinction.

Models of the kind we have been considering are to this extent based on inappropriate categorization, and they therefore yield false choices for the development strategist. A build-up of physical capital, plant and machinery, makes little sense if it is achieved only at the expense of a further deterioration of the workforce which will have to operate it – whereas an improvement in the quality of the workforce (through increased 'consumption') *can* result in higher productivity and therefore increased incomes out of which larger savings may be drawn.

What is ignored in the false strategic dilemmas of investment *versus* consumption, growth *versus* employment and economic *versus* social objectives, are the *dynamic* effects of increased productivity through the betterment of economic conditions, the learning effects of wider employment opportunities, and the incentive spur of enhanced social prospects. It is in these that the seeds of an alternative to the sacrificial theory of development may be discovered.

4. Machines or men?

In the early postwar decades, except for a handful of exceptional cases like Denmark and New Zealand, the division between the Rich World and the Poor World was broadly one between industrialized countries and primary producers. Today the small number of Newly Industrialized Countries (NICs), like Taiwan and Brazil, among the developing nations have achieved much higher growth rates than the underdeveloped nations as a whole. It is not surprising therefore that in early development plans great emphasis was put on the need for rapid industrialization. This was not simply due to a naïve view that problems of underdevelopment could

4. Barber, W. J., 'A Critique of Aggregate Accounting Concepts in Underdeveloped Areas', in the *Bulletin of the Oxford Institute of Economics and Statistics*, November 1963.

be overcome automatically, merely by imitating the production patterns of rich countries. A number of specific arguments were put forward to support the case for substantially increasing the manufacturing sector of a developing economy. It was seen, firstly, as the key to the employment problem: with traditional agriculture already overmanned, where else could jobs be found for the increases in the workforce brought about by the population explosion? Secondly, industrialization was the road to higher productivity: with its greater scope for technological innovation and its susceptibility to economies of large-scale production, manufacturing looked a far more promising bet than agricultural improvements. Thirdly, industrialization could be an instrument for transforming traditional attitudes which had hitherto impeded development: contact with new techniques and radically different working and social environments would widen horizons and foster the development-orientated drives which had been lacking in the past. And finally, there were strong external reasons for stressing the importance of industrial development: the need to reduce dependence on the export of a few primary products for which long-term prospects were gloomily uncertain, and the importance of creating domestic substitutes for manufactured imports in face of balance of payments difficulties.

The share of new investment going to the manufacturing sector in underdeveloped countries was therefore commonly in excess of that channelled into agriculture. Manufacturing output has consequently grown rapidly – indeed, as can be seen from the table below, faster than it has in industrialized countries.

The effect has been to increase substantially the proportion of the gross domestic products of the less developed countries which is derived from manufacturing industry. It still accounts for 14 per cent of total output in low income developing countries; but in middle income countries it is 20 per cent, compared with 24 per cent in industrial nations.

The arguments in favour of industrialization are strong ones; and no doubt one of the key elements in long-run development is that poor countries do diversify their economies by encouraging manufacturing industry. However, it is still open to question, firstly, whether underdeveloped countries have *over*-concentrated on industrialization to the neglect of other basic development

15. Average annual growth rate of manufacturing, 1970–82 (per cent)	
Low income countries	3·4
Middle income countries	5·5
Industrial market economies	2·4

Source: World Bank, op. cit.

requirements (the subject of the next section); and secondly, whether industrialization so far has taken the most suitable *form*. There are many aspects to this second question such as the issues of public versus private enterprise, and inward-looking (import substitution) versus outward-looking (export promotion) emphasis in developing manufacturing industries.

In this section, we shall concentrate on just one aspect of the debate. Have poor countries been wise in their *choice of techniques* and in their equation of industrialization with urban concentration? Doubt that this is so stems, above all, from the disappointing contribution which industrialization has so far made in solving the mounting unemployment problem. The evidence is of two pessimistic trends: firstly, that employment in manufacturing industry has grown a great deal more slowly than output in that sector; and secondly, that industrial employment has not kept pace with the rise in the total workforce. In other words, the *proportion* of workers engaged in manufacturing industry in underdeveloped countries is actually falling – and industrialization is failing to absorb increases in the workforce, let alone deal with the backlog problem of existing open unemployment.

One of the themes of this book is the extent to which the cards are stacked against late developers. In a variety of ways, development was easier in the nineteenth century than it is today. However, it can be argued that there are some *advantages* in starting late. One is the fact that the technology for industrialization has already been created. The industrial histories of present underdeveloped countries will not have to include catalogues of the Great Inventions such as those which fill accounts of our own industrial revolution. For that job has already been done by the now rich countries. Know-how about products, techniques and processes is already available. All that poor countries today have to do is to *apply* the accumulated stock of knowledge.

Unfortunately, it is not quite so straightforward. Modern western-type technology has features which make it only very dubiously applicable in underdeveloped economies. Current techniques used in advanced economies are the result of lengthy scientific developments spanning two centuries. They are extremely sophisticated and require, therefore, correspondingly specialist co-operant skills and attitudes. And above all, the technology is capital-intensive. It is the product of economies in which physical capital is relatively abundant and in which labour is in relatively short supply. It involves a set of techniques which deliberately aims at economizing on the use of manpower. How appropriate is it to the radically different conditions which exist in poor countries?

There *is* an economic case to be made out for consciously opting for a capital-biased path to development. Once again, it rests on the savings-centred theory of growth which was criticized in the last section. Projects using large quantities of capital, it is argued, are those yielding a high ratio of profits to wages. And whereas wages are likely to be spent on consumption, profits will be ploughed back into still further capital accumulation. Industrialization along capital-intensive lines will therefore result in a higher rate of growth in the economy. Then again, although underdeveloped countries have plentiful labour, it is mostly of low quality. Particular managerial and technical skills are in short supply. Capital-intensive projects are those which economize in the use of these scarce factors. Admittedly, such a strategy does little to alleviate current unemployment. But, say its advocates, it will make a greater contribution in the long run to the solution of the problem (by building up more quickly the capital stock needed to create jobs) than a policy of using labour-intensive techniques from the start which does nothing to stimulate the growth rate.

It is difficult, in the light of the experience of underdeveloped countries in recent years, to retain much credence in such an approach. For one thing, even the limited quantities of co-operant skills necessary to operate modern technology effectively have generally failed to be forthcoming. This has been true of both the executive and boardroom levels, and also on the shop floor. A modern steel mill or motor car assembly plant, for example, is

designed on certain assumptions about labour – that workers have
not only a technical understanding of the processes they perform,
but also certain attitudes – that they will turn up for work regularly
and punctually, and that while they are at work they will operate
at given intensities. The typical workforce of a modern plant in a
poor country is very different. Through lack of background it is
likely to be technically unsympathetic to the capital equipment it
operates (which leads, for instance, to a characteristic lack of
attention to maintenance); continuity and tempo are prone to
disturbance from social interruptions such as weddings, funerals,
festivals and the seasonality of the industrial work supply. Essentially, the techniques are *alien* and often represent too sharp a break
with traditional modes of production for the co-operant labour to
digest easily. The result is that what are in the first place expensive
techniques in terms of their capital–output ratios become even
more so because of inefficient use. Those who doubt the point are
referred to the black comedy of the erection and early operation of
the Indian steel mills.[5]

What is also forgotten is the interdependence of modern technology and large sales. For efficient use, modern plant generally
depends on long production runs based on mass markets. In
affluent economies, supply to some extent creates its own demand.
Workers of high productivity (high, because they are working with
substantial quantities of capital) earn the sort of incomes needed
to buy the output of mass production industries. In contrast, the
proportion of the working force engaged in the modern manufacturing sector in underdeveloped countries is very small. Here is yet
another vicious circle – narrow markets lead to inefficient use of
modern equipment causing high costs and prices which continue
to limit the size of the market ...

And how true is the further assumption that the higher ratio of
profits to wages stemming from a capital-intensive technology leads
to extensive plough-back into additional capital accumulation? It
depends on whether profit-earners *do* save a substantial proportion
of their incomes; and also on whether they then reinvest the
proceeds in productive enterprises. In the typical condition of an
underdeveloped country, neither condition can be guaranteed.

5. Zinkin, T., *Challenge in India*, Chatto & Windus, 1966.

Certainly, this was the mechanism of British nineteenth-century growth. The small-scale capitalists were those whom Keynes described as being 'allowed to call the best part of the cake theirs . . . on the tacit underlying assumption that they consumed very little of it'. But the profit-maker in a poor country is more likely to be akin to his eighteenth-century counterpart in Britain, spending heavily on ostentatious consumption or seeking speculative gain rather than the reward of industrial enterprise.

The capital-intensive approach to industrialization is often emulative – creating a veneer of modernity on the economy which apes the symptoms of western affluence without bringing about the structural transformation of attitudes and institutions which is really needed to foster radical and sustained change. Its effect has been to create that dualism in underdeveloped countries which was described in Part Two, section 2 – the great gulf between the small, privileged modern sector and the masses which continue in their traditional poverty. But the rural section is not wholly untouched by the modernism of the urban industrial concentrations. Traditional craft industries are destroyed through technologically superior competition from the modern section – adding to the growing pool of unemployment which the new industries are unable to absorb.

It used to be argued that dualism represented a healthy stage in the process of development. The existence of modern industry would provide a favourable demonstration of the possibilities of development and gradually absorb the traditional sector – relying for its labour force on workers disgorged through increased productivity in the rural areas. But what in fact happens is more accurately portrayed by E. F. Schumacher as 'a process of mutual poisoning. The establishment of modern industry in a few metropolitan areas tends to kill off competing types of traditional production throughout the countryside, thus causing widespread unemployment or underemployment. The countryside thereupon takes its revenge by mass migration into the metropolitan areas causing them to grow to a totally unmanageable size.'[6]

Barbara Ward's account of the horrifying nature of this revenge

6. Schumacher, E. F., 'Industrialization through "Intermediate technology"', in *Industrialisation in Developing Countries*, ed. R. E. Robinson, 1965, Old Schools, Cambridge; Overseas Studies Committee. o.p. Reprinted in *Leading Issues in Development Economics* by G. M. Meier, New York, OUP, 1970.

sadly remains as accurate today: '... dense, filthy tenements in the old town, a first staging post for rural migrants; here the buildings are high, dirt accumulates on every floor, the staircase walls and lift shafts serve as latrines and drains, every room is infested, rats roam the yards, bugs fall from the broken ceilings. The sour smell of bitter poverty pervades every room and hallway. In winter piercing cold gathers in the dank buildings. Summer allows no respite from the breathless festering heat. There are many names round the world for these shanty towns and slums – *colonias proleterias* in Mexico, *gourbivilles* in Tunis, *bustees* in India, *barriadas* in Peru, *gecekondu* in Turkey, *ranchos* in Venezuela. But they all describe the same thing – the places in which, quite probably, human misery and discomfort reach their most devastating pitch.'[7]

In the nineteenth century, urbanization did act as a crude development agent, siphoning off labour from the traditional rural sector, forcibly reorienting traditional attitudes and serving as a hotbed of opportunities and ideas. But industrialization then *preceded* urbanization. What is happening in underdeveloped countries today is the reverse. Again to quote Barbara Ward: 'cities exist ... ahead of the industrial system, they lack the solid basis of manufacturing jobs which gave cities growing a hundred years ago, for all their grime and misery, a solid basis of economic life. But in the twentieth century the transmission belt is not working, or rather it is working erratically and dangerously. It is pouring the new migrant multitudes not into a potentially viable urban order but into an urban wilderness where opportunities grow less as the millions pile on top of one another and the farms do not feed them or the industries employ them.'[8]

It is disastrous consequences like these which have resulted from imitative development – the grafting of a layer of capital-intensive modernity onto an otherwise unchanged traditional society. But the opposite strategy, industrializing on the basis of maximum *labour*-intensity, is also doomed to failure. The most labour-intensive techniques are the primitive ones, those which have led to the present low productivity of labour. They are those which are essentially work-sharing rather than work-creating, those which

7. Ward, B., 'The Poor World's Cities', in the *Economist*, 6 December 1969.
8. ibid.

have failed in the past to generate surpluses which could ultimately lead to faster development, those in which there is no new learning process taking place.

The answer, to quote Schumacher again, lies in the application of an 'intermediate technology' lying somewhere between the other two. He put it this way: 'If we define the level of technology in terms of "equipment cost per workplace", we can call the indigenous technology (symbolically speaking) a £1-technology while that of the modern West could be called a £1,000-technology. The current attempt of the developing countries, supported by foreign aid, to infiltrate the £1,000-technology into their economies inevitably kills off the £1-technology at an alarming rate, destroying traditional workplaces at a much faster rate than modern workplaces can be created and producing the "dual economy" with its attendant evils of mass unemployment and mass migration.'[9] He then went on to point out the obvious, but neglected, relationship between the level of capital per workplace and the level of income per worker: 'The average annual income per worker and the average capital per workplace in the developed countries appear to stand in a relationship of roughly 1:1. This implies, in general terms, that it takes one man-year to create one workplace, or that a man would have to save one month's earnings a year for twelve years to be able to buy his own workplace. If the relationship were 1:10, it would require ten man-years to create one workplace, and a man would have to save a month's earnings a year for 120 years before he could make himself independent. This, of course, is an impossibility, and it follows that the £1,000-technology transplanted into a country the bulk of which is stuck on the level of the £1-technology simply cannot spread by any process of normal growth ... Its "demonstration effect" is wholly negative. The vast majority of people, to whom the £1,000-technology is wholly inaccessible, simply "give up".'[10] An appropriate technology, on the other hand, would be one which would be 'vastly superior in productivity to their traditional technology (in its present state of decay) while at the same time being vastly cheaper and simpler than the highly sophisticated and enormously capital-intensive technology of the

9. Schumacher (Meier), op. cit. p. 357.
10. ibid.

West. As a general guide it may be said that this "intermediate technology" should be on the level of £70–£100 per equipment cost per average workplace. At this level it would stand in a tolerably realistic relationship to the annual income obtainable by an able worker outside the westernized sectors ...'[11]

This certainly offers a more promising line of development than that which has been generally followed during the postwar years. Given the limited capital stock of an underdeveloped country, then *obviously* only relatively few 'modern' workplaces can be created from it; or, to put it the other way round, the amount of investment needed to provide modern workplaces for the whole workforce would be astronomically beyond the reach of any poor country. But that is not the only point. Any technology, to be well operated, must be one which can be learnt and applied by the existing workforce. In the case of the early developers, the so-called 'Great Inventions' were in fact only relatively minor improvements on what had gone before and were therefore digestible by a working population which remained largely untrained and illiterate. Moreover, the way was open for small-scale entrepreneurs to build up modest amounts of capital and seize the profitable opportunities which development offered. In contrast, western technology applied to present poor countries involves a massive adjustment of working attitudes and practices if the alien techniques are to be effectively used. And its demonstration effect, as Schumacher noted, tends to be negative rather than positive. Finally, too, the £1,000-technology is one which has to be largely imported – a further call on limited foreign exchange earnings.

But is a set of intermediate techniques readily available? One possible source lies in the pool of technical experience built up by the now developed countries in the past. Rich countries in their own development passed through many stages – at which the techniques which they used varied enormously. There is thus a wide *range* of technologies on which underdeveloped countries can draw. Might it therefore be possible for them to apply some of these earlier techniques, at least in a suitably adapted form? There have been examples of this happening: 'The Greek shipping industry is one of the world's biggest and works extensively with second-hand ships. Mexico started her steel industry with old US equipment and recently bought US military surplus supplies to construct a shipyard. Brazil has also made extensive use of old equipment. Unfortunately these seem to be isolated examples, and some countries such as India and Pakistan have even prohibited the import of used equipment.'[12]

Beyond this there are two possibilities in the development of an intermediate technology. One is the adaptation of modern western techniques to a labour-surplus situation – hardly a promising approach since it has been specifically designed to diametrically opposite requirements. And the other is that such techniques should be newly invented. Both imply that developing countries must themselves devise new approaches, rather than merely rely on the accumulated know-how of developed countries. And both imply the need for a research and development effort on a scale which has yet to be faced up to.

Such an effort is urgently called for because the potential benefits of intermediate technology are considerable. It offers the only immediate prospect of coming to grips with the overwhelming problem of worklessness. It involves types of capital equipment of which a substantial proportion might be produced indigenously rather than being imported from abroad. It is a technology which makes possible a *dispersed* location of industry – to serve as a basis for 'rural renaissance' rather than the present wasteful and squalid urban concentrations of industry. And it is an approach which will create positive demonstration effects, through which the possibility and potentialities of change can be readily seen, so that development can become a genuinely participatory process with substantial 'spread' effects.

Why, then, have underdeveloped countries persisted in equating industrialization with the erection of prestigious but inappropriate imitations of modern technology? There exists a powerful coalition of interests which impedes the search for more relevant techniques. There are, on the one hand, politicians and planners in underdeveloped countries, biased by an urban and a western outlook in which the 'progressiveness' of the policies is measured by industrial

12. Maddison, A., *Economic Progress and Policy in Developing Countries*, Allen & Unwin, 1970, p. 182.

symbols of modernity. They may be deeply resentful of any suggestion that less developed countries should be 'fobbed off' with
techniques 'inferior' to those used in the west. And the rich countries, on the other hand, are eager accomplices. It is certainly in
their interest to promote the use of capital-intensive technologies;
for it is precisely this sort of equipment that underdeveloped
countries are least likely to produce for themselves, and which the
rich countries are geared to provide. Aid and private investment
have therefore also played a part in foisting on to poor countries
techniques inappropriate to their situation.

An unholy identity of interests between those who dictate the
course of development in poor countries and those who provide
some of the wherewithal thus impedes the emergence of an industrialization strategy which could create a general economic advance
rather than the superficial gloss of dualism.

5. Rural regeneration

Poor countries continue to be the hewers of wood and the drawers
of water in the world economy. The great bulk of the population
of the underdeveloped world earns its living from farming. The
international pattern of production still follows the lines of the
division of labour which was imposed during the nineteenth century, with the rich countries concentrating on the output of manufactured goods which they then trade for raw materials produced
by poor primary producers. As we shall see in Part Four, this
division of labour is one which is profoundly biased against less
developed countries. The greater opportunities for productivity
increase in manufacturing industry and the poor long-term demand
prospects for primary products combine to make trade between
the two groups of countries a further disequalizing force.

Recognition that this was so, led many poor countries to regard
industrialization as synonymous with development. But, as we
have just seen, overemphasis on an inappropriate form of industrialization has had disastrous consequences. A naïve priority stress
on western-type industry has made nonsense of their development
programmes. However imperative it is that underdeveloped countries ultimately diversify their economies to reduce dependence on
a handful of primary products, agriculture continues to play a

number of vital short- and medium-term roles. To neglect these is to court the danger of aborting the whole development effort.

The first function of the rural sector is to provide a food supply. This may seem so obvious as hardly to need stressing. What do need spelling out, however, are the dimensions of the task. The demands made on agricultural producers in underdeveloped countries are generally very considerable indeed. In the first place, food has to be found to match increases in the population – commonly round about 2 per cent per annum. On top of this, output per farm worker has to be boosted to meet the needs of a rapidly swelling urban population. And finally, more food is needed to raise present dietary standards to acceptable and indeed economic levels. Together, these require a rapid and sustained growth in agricultural productivity year after year.

There are also a variety of ways in which the rural sector is crucially linked to the industrial sector – so that successful industrialization depends closely on parallel development of agriculture. It can be seen as the market for industrial output – consumer goods, agricultural equipment, fertilizers and pesticides. It is a source of inputs for the industrial sector – of both raw materials and labour. However unreliable and depressing the long-run prospects, primary production continues for the time being to be the major earner of foreign exchange available in most underdeveloped economies. And it is also a main source of domestic capital accumulation.

There are two further reasons for emphasizing the fundamental strategic significance of rural development. The first concerns employment. We have already seen that manufacturing industry is likely to make only a relatively small contribution towards solving the problem of rapidly rising unemployment. Positive rural policies are required, not to release labour for absorption in urban industry, but to create work for the growing joblessness.

And perhaps most important of all, rural progress is vital because that is where the people happen to be. To be meaningful, development must be a participatory process in which the masses are involved and moved. So much of what is commonly termed development – generally measured by increases in national income – is really nothing of the sort, affecting as it does only small groups of people concentrated in a handful of urban areas. If development is to include a general widening of horizons, and if its benefits are to be widely dispersed, then substantial resources *must* be directed into the rural section.

But if it is in agriculture that change is most urgently needed – because present productivity both per person and per acre are so meagre in relation to growing demands – it is the countryside which is at the same time most *resistant* to change. Farmers the world over tend to be conservative, and in underdeveloped countries the rural population represents the very kernel of traditional society in which practices are hallowed by generations of time and in which innovations are therefore regarded with the deepest suspicion.

Outside observers often view the problems of transforming traditional agriculture from one of two extreme positions. For some, the peasants in underdeveloped countries are simply a different breed of economic animal from their western counterparts – ignorant, obstinate, contented with their present lot, and therefore unresponsive to the usual economic stimuli. If they do respond at all, it is perversely. For example, they will react to increased prices by *cutting* rather than expanding production – because the higher prices enable them to earn their previous income with less effort. Against this gloomy view of the human obstacles to rural change can be set the over-optimism of the agricultural technocrats. 'Expertism', as we could label this approach, sees the solution essentially in terms of introducing new techniques rather than in changing human attitudes and institutional structures.

The dangers of 'expertism', the indiscriminate advocacy of methods successful in quite different conditions elsewhere, are enormous. The damage which can be caused by the transfer of inappropriate agrarian techniques is as great as that which we have already discussed with regard to the industrial sector. Take, for example, the process of mechanization. Agriculture in developed economies is high-yielding. It is also highly mechanized. It is easy to conclude that the solution to poor-country problems is therefore to introduce modern machines which can combine with local labour to increase output. The potentially disastrous results of this approach can be illustrated by the history of one such well-meaning experiment. With American help, the Turkish government during the post-war period embarked on a programme of mechanization to revolutionize traditional agriculture. 'The number of tractors in

Turkey increased from 1,756 in 1948 to 44,144 in 1957. Roughly a third of these tractors were used in central Anatolia to clear and cultivate marginal land previously used for livestock. The mechanization of production had two effects. First, over-grazing on the remaining pasture was accentuated, over-cultivation of the new lands was encouraged, and erosion was accelerated. Secondly, mechanization increased the number of unemployed. It has been estimated that each tractor displaced an average of eight people, and between 1950 and 1955 about 350,000 workers were forced to become migrants. Heavy expenditure on roads – like the tractors, largely financed with foreign aid – encouraged internal migration. Investment in highways rose from TL65 million in 1950 to TL943 million in 1960. The government having created technological unemployment and having done nothing to raise agricultural yields, the peasants simply used the new roads to leave rural areas. The major effect of investing in new tractors and roads was to increase the number of unemployed and to expand the urban slums.[13]

Similar examples of misplaced expertism abound in many other parts of the world. In the Turkish case, the large-scale introduction of tractors destroyed the ecological balance and disgorged labour for which no alternative employment existed. More generally, it is also inappropriate for other reasons: firstly, the heavy foreign exchange cost of imported machinery; secondly, a corresponding need for foreign exchange over the life of the machines to pay for necessary replacement components; and thirdly, the need for skills in driving and maintaining the machines – skills which are frequently lacking. Tractors lie rusting in many parts of the underdeveloped world as testimony to the dangers of expertism.

There is perhaps a small lesson from history to be learned here. The British agricultural revolution which played such a crucial role in British economic development was really not very revolutionary if judged by the new techniques which underlaid it. What were those techniques? Certainly not tractors and combine harvesters. One important innovation was the seed drill – a simple device for sowing seeds in straight lines rather than broadcasting them. This in turn enabled the deployment of another new tool – the horse-hoe – to make extensive weeding possible. Certainly there was a

13. Griffin and Enos, op. cit., pp. 137–8.

good deal more to the agrarian transformation of Britain than this (particularly new crop rotations and the structural reform brought about by the enclosure movement). But the new techniques themselves were relatively simple and therefore easy to understand and accept.

Similarly, although technical change is certainly a necessary ingredient in transforming the traditional agriculture of underdeveloped countries today, the need for *appropriate* techniques is as great as in industrial development. And one of the great advantages of agriculture is its scope for the application of relatively labour-intensive technology. Dramatic improvements can be brought about with only modest injections of capital – if the farmer can only be persuaded to change his ways.

Why are the farmers so loath to accept innovations which they are assured will make them better off? To some extent, it must be a case of a bird in the hand being worth more than two in the bush. Their traditional methods have at least been *proved* by generations of practice. This is a point stressed by Leonard Joy: 'In many parts of the underdeveloped world there are farmers with a deep practical understanding of their farming environment ... It is a mistake to think that because poor-country farming systems use primitive tools and techniques they are therefore simple ... The peasant farmer's reputation for conservatism reflects in large measure scientists' frustrations in their attempts to improve peasant farming. In many instances the peasant farmer's reputation is unwarranted; the facts show scientists to be offering correct but irrelevant information.'[14]

What is often mistaken for obstinacy on the part of such farmers is in fact a shrewd assessment on their part of the dubious value of proposed innovations in the local circumstances which they understand far better than the experts themselves. The answer is often said to lie in provision of agricultural extension services which can bring home to the farmer an appreciation of new opportunities, and relate new methods to local conditions. This is a great deal easier said than done. For, to be effective, agricultural advisory services must permeate throughout the countryside and be particu-

14. Joy, L., 'Strategy for Agricultural Development', in *Development in a Divided World*, ed. by Dudley Seers and Leonard Joy, Penguin Books, 1971, pp. 175–7.

larly active at the village level. The agricultural extension workers must themselves be technically well versed in the new techniques and they must be able to demonstrate to suspicious and sceptical farmers that they really do work – by, for example, applying them in model farms where conditions are the same as those faced by the local peasants. Ideally, then, they are people of remarkable qualities combining the roles of agronomist, practical farmer, diplomat and salesman. Any country with a plentiful supply of such personnel is unlikely to be an underdeveloped one. Typically, it is precisely these skills which are scarce – and just people with such qualities who are most reluctant to make their careers in the unrewarding rural areas. Partly this is the result of the urban bias of the educational system which commonly characterizes underdeveloped countries. But whatever the reason, the unfortunate result is that local extension workers are often unconvincing and inefficient and fail to make any real impression on local practices.

Again, there is no point in persuading farmers of the value of new methods – and then failing to provide them with the wherewithal to put them into effect. The necessary inputs must be made available in the right quantities, in the right place and at the right time. Frequently, improvement schemes have come to grief because of failures to back up effectively the diffusion of new techniques by the provision of the requirements to make them work. For example, application of chemical fertilizers without plentiful water can cause crop-burning. Irrigation without adequate drainage can lead to salination of the soil. It takes only an occasional disastrous episode of this kind to confirm farmers in the wisdom of their cautious conservatism and to set them even more firmly in their traditional ways.

The life of tropical peasant farmers is normally a very hard one, fraught with natural hazards of all kinds. What they have learned to do, above all, is to insure themselves against risks as far as possible. Offer them the choice between a traditional technique which in a bad year will give them 50 bushels per acre and 75 in a good year, and a modern method which might yield 125 but which might also, in unfavourable conditions, produce only 25 – and they are bound to opt for the safer outcome. Only when the new methods are shown to be no more risky than the old will the farmers finally be won over.

And yet despite all these problems, a dramatic change did take place in agriculture in underdeveloped countries during the sixties. Quite suddenly, output in many areas sharply increased. This was due to the introduction of new seed varieties of wheat, maize and rice developed in Mexico and the Philippines. The great merit of these new strains is that they allow much heavier dosage of fertilizers than the traditional varieties. A doubling or tripling of yields was thereby made possible through this Green Revolution. Food production in developing countries increased by 2·9 per cent between 1960 and 1970 and by 2·8 per cent in the decade to 1980 – even slightly ahead of population growth.

The overall prospects for achieving greater self-reliance in food production have thus certainly increased. But there remains considerable and often growing dependence on the outside world. As the Brandt Report has pointed out, 'the developing countries have rapidly increased their imports of cereals, from relatively low levels in the 1950s, to 20 million tonnes in 1960 and 1961, to over 50 million tonnes in the early 1970s, and nearly 80 million by 1978–9.'[15] By 1982 the figure was 96 million tonnes. Moreover, the potential gains from the scientific breakthroughs have been far from evenly dispersed. For example, in 24 African countries grain production per person has actually fallen by 2 per cent a year since 1970.

The point made previously needs emphasizing again: the new seed varieties need large inputs of fertilizers which in turn means plentiful water. Both require capital. In practice, therefore, the strains can only be adopted by a relatively small number of already progressive and prosperous farmers. The great mass of peasant farmers remain untouched. In parallel with the urban/rural inequalities caused by urban bias in development planning, the Green Revolution has served to widen rural inequalities. Little has happened to alter the attitude and opportunities of the great rural masses. A genuine agricultural revolution must mean more than this. As Mrs Judith Hart warned the 1969 FAO General Conference: 'Development must not result in prosperous farmers growing richer while peasants grow poorer; those displaced by agricultural development must not become the new urban unemployed; those

15. *North–South: A Programme for Survival*, report of the Independent Commission on International Development Issues, chaired by Willy Brandt, Pan, 1980, p. 91.

most in need of food must have the opportunity to buy it.' It must be doubted how far the Green Revolution has served to achieve any of these ends.

Apart from research into new techniques and the dissemination of new knowledge, what incentives should be provided to induce farmers to adopt them? One possibility is that they should be *taxed* into more progressive methods. If taxes are set sufficiently high, then to maintain their own consumption farmers will have to increase output for the market in order to pay their taxes. This in essence is the policy followed by Japan in the late nineteenth and early twentieth centuries, with the peasant being ruthlessly squeezed to provide a surplus for capital accumulation. But quite apart from the political and practical infeasibility of such a strategy in most parts of the underdeveloped world today, such an approach is open to two criticisms. Is the continued impoverishment of the rural sector a satisfactory base for the development of urban industries which may be dependent on it as an outlet for its goods? And what sort of 'development' is this anyway in which the part of the economy in which the great mass of people live is deliberately kept at a low standard of living?

An alternative set of incentives is that provided by the market mechanism. To induce farmers to produce more, offer them higher prices for their output. Certainly, there seems to be little positive evidence for a traditional view that peasant farmers have a 'backward sloping supply curve', i.e. that when offered higher prices they will respond by *reducing* rather than increasing production since they are now able to earn the same income for a smaller amount of effort. But there are other problems associated with price incentives. One is that high prices for farmers means increased cost of living for urban workers – with consequent cost-push inflationary effects (unless rationing or subsidies can be effectively implemented). And the other is that, once again, it is the already progressive and relatively prosperous farmers who are most likely to be able to capitalize on price incentives. If development implies that the great mass of the rural population are to participate, then price policy on its own is not going to do the trick. However, to the extent that prices are used, it is important to supplement the policy by measures to provide more incentive goods. Farmers are unlikely to be bothered about earning more money unless they have the opportunity of spending it on desirable goods. In a remote village bounded by tradition there may not seem much point in trying to increase income.

We have been looking at a variety of ways in which traditional agriculture can be improved. But it must be doubted how effective any of them can be without complementary changes in the basic structure of traditional farming. So far we have been discussing innovations *within* the present institutional structure. But can these be effective without altering the parameters of the system itself – the size of farm and the basis of tenure or ownership on which it is worked? The problem varies from country to country and region to region. In some the average size of plot is too small to act as a viable development unit. In others, land is concentrated in a very few hands. But the problem is only partly one of creating farms of an appropriate size. It is also one of ensuring that those prepared to make agricultural improvements are rewarded for doing so. Absentee landlordism, sharecropping, landlessness – all add up to a situation in which there is little opportunity or incentive for the rural masses to stir themselves.

Land reform is thus, in many underdeveloped countries, a prerequisite for sustained growth of agricultural productivity and the only basis on which a genuine agricultural revolution can be promoted. But it is also one of the most difficult of institutional changes to bring about. For it is at this point that anti-development interests are most powerful. Most poor countries pay lip-service to the notion of land reform, and many have complex legislation in their statute books ostensibly aimed at achieving it. And yet commonly it is a sham. Legal ceilings on the size of landholding in India, for example, have merely led to a nominal redistribution of land between members of a family with nothing basically changed. Ways of evading land reform legislation have not been difficult to find, particularly when landowners have realized that governments have been concerned more with paper revolution rather than real change. New seed varieties, foreign food aid and the like have often served only to make it possible for governments in poor countries to avoid that basic confrontation with powerful agricultural interests which agrarian development really demands.

It perhaps needs stressing once again that the object of increasing agricultural efficiency is *not* to release surplus labour for deployment in a rapidly growing urban industrial workforce. Urban employment is failing even to absorb the natural increase in the working population, let alone that made redundant by the application of capital-intensive techniques in agriculture. In any case, it is a fallacy to believe that the rural sector is heavily 'underemployed', if by that is meant that workers can be siphoned off without any fall in output. With *given* techniques and attitudes, evidence suggests that farm output can only be maintained with the present number of workers – who are essentially *seasonally* underemployed. Increasing agricultural productivity means introducing the fundamental changes which we have just been discussing, and there is no substitute for them.

No, what is now called for is not merely an agricultural revolution but comprehensive *rural development*. This means, first of all, accepting that the rural sector is the major source of future employment opportunities. It means enhancing the quality of rural life to reverse the present migration to the towns. It is in the countryside that jobs must be created; and it is the countryside which must be revitalized to counter the spurious attractions of the urban slums.

To choose between urban industrialization and rural agriculture is false. For one thing, the industrial and agricultural sectors are deeply interdependent, with the success of each depending on the prosperity of the other. The concept of rural development takes this interdependence a stage further – for it involves shifting the locus of industry out of the squalid and socially expensive urban complexes and into the countryside itself. It aims at reducing the traditional dependence of the rural areas on a few primary products by diversifying production into a host of labour-biased non-agricultural activities.

The range of possibilities which could be opened up by such an approach is indicated by some examples taken from the discussion by Griffin and Enos of ways of 'industrializing agriculture'. They stress the point that 'the provision of food transformation industries is anyway often an *essential element in a programme of agricultural change*. Expansion of the output of tomatoes, for example, might be wasteful unless a canning factory were near by to prevent spoilage. Investment in a dairy herd might be unprofitable unless a farm has access to milk, butter, cheese and ice-cream industries. Production of sugar-cane would be more rewarding if a refinery were available. An increase in pig-raising would be difficult without a slaughterhouse and a meat-packing industry, etc. Industrial investment, far from being an alternative to agriculture, may in some cases be highly complementary to it. There are also considerable opportunities for developing industries which provide inputs to the agricultural sector. Modest establishments to manufacture and repair simple agricultural implements will be required at first. Later, more complex machinery and metal working industries will be needed to provide such things as motor-drawn rakes, and eventually tractors. A quite separate industrial complex could be based on the chemical industry and the provision of fertilizers. A third complex could focus on supplying the sector with fuels and other petroleum products . . .'[16]

On top of this, there exists enormous scope for the employment of the seasonally underemployed in building, using labour-intensive methods, a new rural infrastructure of roads, schools and houses. The potential gains from vigorous rural development are very great indeed. That they continue to be widely neglected is at least partly due to an urban bias in development planning stemming from a set of educational values which sees the persistence of a rural way of life as the hallmark of failure.

6. Schools for progress

The ability of a society to provide more and better education for its members can be regarded as one of the objectives of economic development. But as well as being an *end* of development, it can also be a significant instrument in achieving it.

Newly independent countries understandably stressed education in their development plans as a vital feature of the just societies which it was their declared intention to create. Particularly since the metropolitan powers had done little in this field, the goal of national education was a logical extension of the independence struggle. Availability of education was seen as a basic human right, a freeing of people's minds parallel to the achievement of political independence from colonial bondage.

Then again, as has been discussed in other sections, the emphasis

16. Griffin and Enos, op. cit., pp. 139–40.

in early development plans on the need for increased physical investment soon became tempered by recognition that modern capital equipment is of little use without the appropriate human skills to work it effectively. It therefore became fashionable, in developed as well as underdeveloped countries, to stress the importance of a build-up of *human* capital. Education was investment in people – a sacrifice of immediate consumption in order to create a more productive workforce in the future.

Expenditure on education could therefore be defended on grounds both of humanity and economic efficiency. Consequently there have been spectacular increases in expenditure on education in developing countries to the point where it now comprises some 9 per cent of their governments' spending (much more than the 5 per cent on average of the budgets of governments in the developed countries), and impressive figures can be produced to show the growth of enrolments at the primary and secondary stages.

However, what such aggregate figures (which are anyway highly unreliable) conceal is the qualitative nature of the education which is being provided – and both from the humanitarian and economic standpoints, questions of who is being educated, how, and where, are of crucial importance.

The view that *any* education must promote social justice and economic development is, of course, a naïve one. Education *can* work as a further disequalizing social factor and serve to weaken development impulses rather than to strengthen them. There are a number of biases in the educational programmes of underdeveloped countries which suggest that this has all too frequently been the case.

To a considerable extent these biases are a legacy from the colonial era. This was a period in which the great mass of people received no formal education at all. 'We know that colonial regimes inhibited the development of human resources. In 1911, there were 66,000 British in the Indian army and 4,000 in the civil government. At that time, there were only sixty Indians in the top rank of the civil service and even fewer Indian officers in the army. Foreign investors were also reluctant to develop local technical and managerial competence. Privileged employment opportunities were reserved for nationals of the metropolitan country. Thus they blocked Indian access to managerial skills in large-scale commerce, shipping, railways, banking and jute. A quarter of the managerial personnel in the Indian textile industry in the 1920s were foreigners supplied by the managing agencies. In Egypt the Suez Canal Company did not use Egyptian pilots; in Ceylon and Malaya, most of the supervisory personnel in plantation agriculture were expatriates until relatively recently. The opportunities for local people were even worse in Belgian, Dutch and French colonies than they were in these British-controlled countries.'[17]

Where it served the metropolitan interest to provide education at all, it was on a limited basis for particular groups. Traditional elites were inculcated with the ideals and values of their colonial masters – generations of rich aristocratic Indians, for example, spent their formative years in the public schools and ancient universities of Britain. At a lower level, colonial administrations required a supply of indigenous personnel capable of performing clerical and lower managerial tasks. And finally, there was the stratum of missionary schools where basic education could be obtained at the price of conversion to an alien faith. At all levels it was, of course, the western tradition which was imposed – 'theoretical, humanistic and aristocratic, favouring excellence and original thought rather than mass education ... In the British sphere of influence it was the *Oxbridge Dilettante* and, in French, the *Sorbonne Littérateur* and the lawyer nurtured on Roman and Classical law, who took the pride of place in society and administration. The Dutch and peninsular-dominated world followed a similar course and administrative careers were the only way to fame and wealth, unless one belonged to one of the great feudal landowning or merchant prince families.'[18]

Astonishingly, political independence has generally been followed by a reinforcement of this western bias in education rather than a reaction away from it. The old values have commonly been inherited wholesale and used as a basis for wider educational programmes.

The essence of the western, and in particular the British liberal approach to education is that it should produce the 'well-rounded' individual who has been taught how to learn rather than trained in

17. Maddison, op. cit., pp. 23–4.
18. Balogh, op. cit., p. 176.

specific skills. And the means of creating such all-round amateurs, it
has always been felt, is primarily through the humanities. It is a
tradition which shuns the vocational approach. Those trained in
the sciences and technology are regarded as narrow and limited;
they seldom before the war achieved top positions in government
or business management. Ironically, in the older developed countries, it has now been recognized that such attitudes are not those
most conducive to rapid economic growth, but instead 'conspire
to defeat industrial dynamism ... The trouble with the public
school and Oxbridge graduates lies not in the "old-boy" network
of recruitment but rather in their amateurism and their frequent
acceptance of business as a second choice when they fail to qualify
for a civil service career. They tend to retain the civil service as their
model and settle into a trustee role of gentlemanly responsibility
that hardly conduces to rapid innovation.'[19] In Britain, concern
about a disappointing growth performance has led to strenuous
efforts being made to achieve a more balanced educational output.

Unfortunately, the ideal of the gifted dilettante continues to
flourish in many underdeveloped countries. At the primary and
secondary levels, it is the formal 'grammar school' approach which
dominates the curriculum. In the universities, it is the faculties of
the arts subjects, law and medicine, which frequently still cream
off the undergraduate intake. There may yet be some truth in the
Muggeridge dictum that 'the last Englishman will be an Indian'.

Such an educational approach can be immensely harmful in
creating attitudes which are basically anti-development. For the
peasant farmer, 'progress' comes to mean securing sufficient
schooling for his son to get him off the land and into an urban
office job. The career priorities of graduates closely reflect the
status hierarchies as they existed in the colonial period: first, a post
in the higher echelons of the civil service; second best, an executive
position with a foreign-owned company; thirdly teaching, prefer-
ably at university level, and certainly town-based. Their preferences
are encouraged by salary differentials also inherited from the past.
But development is a process requiring both specific skills and
dynamic attitudes, and whatever the intrinsic worth of a humanities
education there is no evidence to suggest that these are the qualities

19. Caves, R. E., ed., *Britain's Economic Prospects*, Allen & Unwin, 1968, p. 303.

which it produces. The present pattern of education not only does nothing to promote development; it may positively impede it. For it involves a bias towards manipulation rather than *doing*. It creates a vested interest in the maintenance of the comfortable *status quo* and makes for a reluctance (together with inability) to face up to the painful choices involved in development.

If the promotion of economic development and social justice are its aims, then the type of education needed is radically different from the present one. Priority would first of all have to be given to programmes of mass literacy – both as a human right and also as a precondition for the evolution of a successful development ideology. Admittedly, in the case of many early developers, economic growth preceded universal education by several generations. But that does not mean that present poor countries should follow the same path. To some extent it is simply not possible for them to do so – because of the much higher levels of skills demanded by present technologies. In any case, the example is irrelevant because early development was spontaneous and unplanned. Now, when it is the task of development planners deliberately to create the conditions necessary for development, a genuine participatory movement can only be generated if mass communication is possible. And what needs stressing in this respect is the importance of spreading literacy not just to future generations but also to the present one. *Adult* education, largely neglected in most programmes, has a crucial contribution to make. A dramatic example of what is possible in this area is the Cuban achievement (noted not only by those politically sympathetic) in reducing illiteracy from 23·6 per cent to 3·9 per cent within a year. 'Not a miracle,' as a UNESCO report commented, 'but rather a difficult conquest obtained through work, techniques and organization.'[20]

'The formal objective was literacy and a national campaign for eight months was launched to achieve it. By the end of the campaign, nearly a million adult illiterates – about a fifth of the adult population – had been enrolled and over 700,000, it was claimed, had acquired basic literacy. But the campaign's importance ... lies more in its effects on the attitudes and commitment of the hundreds and thousands of people involved. These indirect effects on

20. Inter-American Development Bank, Washington, 1967, p. 31.

attitudes were probably more significant even than the campaign's
formal achievement in teaching so many persons to read and write.
A virtual army of 106,000 teenagers, mostly from the towns, had
been organized to live for eight months in the country. Each stayed
with a peasant, helping with farm work and, for two hours a day,
teaching him to read and write. In the towns another 100,000
adults – secretaries, government workers, businessmen and dust-
men – were doing the same, teaching illiterates two hours a day
in the lunch-hour or after work. The effects of this intimate
involvement – bridging the gulf between rural and urban areas,
crossing social barriers, differences of occupation, of age and ways
of life – made a profound impression on human attitudes. This, to
the common man, *was* revolution.'[21] Richard Jolly, in this account
of the 1961 literacy campaign in Cuba, stresses not just the instrumental value of literacy as a precondition for the acquisition
of further skills and learning, but also its role in creating new
development-oriented attitudes. Moreover, it represented the first
fruits of development and provided evidence that it meant change
for the better. More recently, in the spring and summer of 1980,
100,000 students and school children in Nicaragua went into the
countryside to teach the *campesinos* how to read and write. It is
claimed that in less than six months the illiteracy rate fell from
55 per cent to 14 per cent of the population, as half a million
Nicaraguans learned to read and write.

If education is to act as an instrument of development policy it
must be purged of its present overwhelming urban bias and disdain
for the practical. All too frequently in underdeveloped countries,
the values which young people absorb at school and at university
lead them to regard work in the rural sector as the hallmark of
failure – and to seek, above all, employment which involves no
dirtying of the hands. Such attitudes are cultivated not only by the
educational system but also by the general development strategy
(which in turn, of course, is determined by products of that
education) – equating development with industrialization, and
overstressing the urban sector at the expense of the rural areas in
which the mass of the people happen to live.

21. Jolly, R., 'Manpower and Education', in *Development in a Divided World*,
op. cit., pp. 214–15.

There is an urgent need for a schooling system in most under-developed countries which is 'a useful introduction rather than a perpetual deterrent to rural life'. Such a system implies a sharp break from traditional modes of teaching. Part-time education interspersed with periods of work on model extension farms, the rooting of the curriculum in rural requirements such as the importance of hygiene and nutrition, elementary crop management and other aspects of rural science, all have a part to play in relating education directly to improved productivity in the rural sector. But they are unlikely in themselves to stem the townward migration of the young unless they are embodied in a general strategy of rural development along the lines which we have already discussed.

Similarly, technical training at all levels must receive far more emphasis than it has in the past. Partly this is a matter of giving it a new status to attract the best rather than the second-rate intake. Partly it is a matter of location – of dispersing technical schools and colleges throughout the country, rather than concentrating them in capital cities. Once again, however, education must be fully integrated in the general development strategy. Many underdevel-oped countries now face an increasing problem of 'educated' unemployed – sometimes even technically educated unemployed. There is little point in increasing the availability of trained personnel unless policy is oriented towards creating job opportunities for them.

And finally, as with industrialization, the *techniques* of education in poor countries have often been slavish imitations of their western counterparts. The school and university buildings, their equipment, the teacher:student ratio, the period of education – are often all modelled on what is acceptable in affluent western societies. In other words, they are 'capital-intensive' techniques. But how much sense does this make in different climatic conditions, and in a poor-country situation where the cost of such techniques – in terms of alternative output foregone – is so much greater? The social cost of training someone to graduate level is substantial even in rich countries. But for an underdeveloped economy, the cost – measured by days of peasant labour – is very much higher. And yet doctors, for example, are still generally trained to the same level and for the same period of time as if they were qualifying in Britain or the United States. And when they complete their training, they practise mostly in the urban areas, saving to set up their own private clinics to administer to the needs of a still narrower but more rewarding clientele. What needs stressing is that 'better means fewer'. A more appropriate approach, to take the case of medicine again, would be to produce a very much larger quantity of rather less highly qualified staff – an approach, pioneered by the Chinese 'barefoot doctors' and now widely followed in other developing countries where paramedics provide primary health care in rural areas. Perhaps a condition of acceptance at a medical school should be that doctors serve minimum stipulated periods in the rural areas where they are needed most. Such proposals sound 'illiberal' to western ears. But the point is, of course, that in affluent societies we can *afford* to be liberal to a greater extent than in a poor country where catering for the demanding requirements of the few is inevitably at the expense of the needier many.

Only with radical reform can education in the majority of underdeveloped countries fulfil its potentially significant role in mobilizing human resources. For the time being, it often serves to create further resistances to change rather than to inculcate a powerful drive towards development.

PART FOUR
THE WORLD OUTSIDE

The international framework in which development now has to take place is profoundly different from that of the nineteenth century. Britain and the other early developers broke through to modern economic growth as the first amongst equals. There was then no group of very much richer countries in the international economy to help or hinder their progress. Poor countries today, in contrast, must pitch their development efforts in the context of a development gap already many generations wide – in an international environment dominated by affluent, economically advanced, industrial nations.

It can be argued that this is an advantage for the late developers. They can learn from the experience of those who have already trodden the development path. From the now rich countries they can draw on a reservoir of scientific, technical and economic knowledge rather than have to create it themselves from scratch. Rich countries can offer prosperous markets for their exports. And poor countries can turn to the more affluent members of the international community for capital and other forms of help.

But in fact the existence of extreme international economic inequalities has worked to increase rather than to reduce the difficulties of the development task. Many of the potential benefits of being late developers have proved to be illusory. The radically different situation faced by developing countries today means that there are disappointingly few lessons to be learned from the past. The pool of accumulated know-how may be inappropriate to their condition – and its indiscriminate application therefore damagingly counter-productive. And the existence of a group of technologically and economically mature countries can have a naturally stifling effect on the development of more backward economies. All this is true even assuming that the rich countries are neutral in their attitude towards development of the poorer three quarters of the world. If they felt threatened by it and wished to limit it, then they are certainly powerful enough to do so. And even if they are genuinely anxious to promote it, their assistance can take misguided forms.

Rich countries certainly *say* that they want to help in the development of poorer parts of the world and to reduce international inequalities. Unfortunately, there is a wide gap between what they say and what they do. The argument of the following sections is that rich countries do have a potentially important role to play in accelerating development. They *could* help – if only to a limited degree since in the last analysis development is essentially an indigenous process. But during the postwar period to date that potential has not been realized. The existence of rich countries has often proved to be a further drag on development, rather than the stimulus which it might have been. This can be seen by looking at the two main areas in which the activities of rich countries impinge on poor ones – the international trade of goods and services, and the movement of resources (capital and labour).

1. Unfair exchange?

In the nineteenth century, international trade was a powerful engine for transmitting growth from one country to another. This was one of the major mechanisms by which other European countries came to emulate the British example – followed later by America and the other lands settled from Europe. The progress of even so late a developer as Japan depended on success in export markets.

The present situation is a very different one. The trading relationship is on the whole between extreme unequals. And secondly it is between rich *industrial* countries and poor *primary* producers. Underdeveloped countries in 1981 earned slightly more from exports of manufactured goods than from sales abroad of food and raw materials. However this reflects the low prices paid for commodities and the higher prices which can be obtained for manufactures. Most of the manufactures were in any case exported by a handful of developing N I Cs, notably Hong Kong, Taiwan and South Korea. The majority of underdeveloped countries remain heavily dependent for their export earnings on sales of raw materials of one kind or another; moreover, most of them are largely reliant on just one or two such products. This is the present international division of labour – a form of specialization which, as was discussed in Part One, was artificially imposed some hundred and fifty years ago.

It was also argued earlier that, once an initial inequality between nations had been established, the simple operation of market forces – without more deliberate exploitation – would serve to widen that gap still farther. The chief way in which the economic distance between nations was increased during the nineteenth century was not one of crude imperial exaction from tributary territories – but the normal working of an ostensibly 'fair' system of free trade. It is time to digress a little and to look at that argument in more detail.

The traditional economic case for free trade suggested that everyone playing the international trade game would benefit from specialization and exchange. Possibly this is true. But the policy conclusion which resulted – that therefore world trade should be maximized by the removal of all barriers to its growth – still only follows if a *world* view is adopted. A simple numerical example may help to make the point clear.

Suppose that there is no international trade to begin with and that the output and income of two countries is as follows:

16. Income and output (before trade)	
Rich country	100
Poor country	10

Now each of them specializes according to its comparative advantage in different lines of production and they exchange the surpluses through international trade. As a result of increased efficiency, they both now achieve a higher level of income and output:

17. Income and output (after trade)	
Rich country	150
Poor country	12

Both have gained from specialization and trade – as the classical economists predicted. And *world* income and output has grown from 110 to 162. But the gains have been very unequally distributed. The richer country has benefited – both in absolute and relative terms – more than the poor country. The gap between them has substantially widened.

Supposing, on the other hand, that the poor country had maintained some barriers to trade so that specialization and trade had been pushed to less than the maximum possible. The result might have been different.

18. Income and output (with limited trade)	
Rich country	110
Poor country	20

Notice the fact that total income and output have now increased by only 20 instead of 52. But both countries in this case secured an increase of 10. The poorer country has gained relatively more than the richer one and the relative gap between them has been reduced (although even here the absolute gap remains unchanged). Obviously, from the point of view of the poor country this is a much preferable situation. But the classical economists, on the other hand, adopted a world perspective in their theories. Beyond predicting that everyone would gain something from trade they neglected the question of the distribution of gains.

Of course, the figures in this example have just been fabricated to suggest what *might* happen. But there are in fact many reasons for supposing that this is just what does happen – that in trade between unequal partners the gains are greater for the richer country than the poorer one.

Look, first of all, at the *basis* of specialization. What happens, according to the theory, is that each country concentrates on that type of production in which it has the greatest comparative advantage. But as we saw earlier, the division of the world into manufacturers and primary producers occurred at a time when the richer countries were able deliberately to stifle competition from peripheral countries. And once such a fundamental division of labour is established, it becomes extraordinarily difficult for the pattern to be changed. Even if tropical countries had a long-term comparative advantage in industrial production, it would be very difficult to demonstrate this in the short run, because attempts to set up manufacturing industries would be aborted by competition from the countries which industrialized earlier.

Traditional economic theory did take this possibility into account. Although tariffs and other obstacles to trade were anathema to the classical economists, an exception was made in the case of so-called 'infant industries'. The theory accepted that while a new industry was being established, a certain amount of protection was necessary – which could later be removed if the anticipated comparative advantage emerged. But the infant industry argument was, and indeed still is, relegated in the textbooks to the status of a minor exception from the golden rule that world welfare is maximized by the general elimination of trading barriers (and it was hedged, too, by warnings that it was a loophole likely to be abused – with cautionary tales of infant industries which never grew up and remained forever heavily protected).

What was not recognized was that this case was more the general rule than the exception – that today three quarters of the world population live in 'infant economies'. Their attempts to diversify from primary production, if they are to succeed in the face of competition from established producers in rich countries, have to be protected.

But even if the present division of labour between manufacturers and primary producers was in the first place an artificial one, is there any real point in disturbing it now? Isn't it a mutually satisfactory state of affairs, with the activities of one group complementing those of the other? Thus as the industrial countries become still richer, they demand more and more materials from poorer countries; the less developed countries thereby earn the foreign currency they need in order to buy manufactured goods from the richer nations.

In reality such a division of labour is a deeply unfair one. Certainly the demand for both primary and manufactured goods will increase as world incomes rise. But they are likely to do so at quite different rates. The rate of growth in demand for primary products is bound to lag seriously behind the increased demand for manufactures.

Primary production is made up of two broad types of commodity – foodstuffs and raw materials. But as your income rises year by year how much of the increase do you spend on food? For most people in this country the answer will be relatively little. The reason is that this is a rich economy in which most of us are lucky enough to have already satisfied our demand for food. As incomes increase beyond a certain point, the proportion of our income which we spend on food declines. Our increased spending is directed more to cars, washing machines, televisions – manufactured consumer goods. In economists' jargon this can be expressed by saying that the *income elasticity of demand* for foodstuffs is lower than that for manufactures.

But what of the raw material element of primary production? Surely that *has* to rise *pari passu* with increased output of manufacturers? For two reasons this is not necessarily so. Firstly, part of the growth process in rich countries is their increasing ability to *economize* in the use of raw materials: they are becoming more efficient partly through managing to squeeze more output out of any given volume of raw materials. And, secondly, rich countries are becoming increasingly adept at inventing and producing substitutes for natural raw materials. Their technological superiority makes it possible to produce an ever-widening range of synthetics to compete against imports from primary producers.

The long-run growth in demand for primary products is therefore likely to be a relatively slow one – a gloomy prospect for those countries which are heavily dependent for their export proceeds on just one or two such products. The matter is made still worse, however, by the fact that rich countries are not solely manufacturing producers. They also produce primary products themselves –

to a far greater extent than poor countries are able to achieve self-sufficiency in manufactures.

The postwar *supply* situation in developing countries compounds the ill-effects of heavy dependence on primary products for which world demand grows only relatively slowly. Development has enabled them substantially to improve agricultural production so that the supply of primary products coming on to world markets has grown rapidly. Coupled with only slowly rising demand, increased supply has forced the world market price of primary products downwards. There is, therefore, a secular tendency at work for the terms of trade of primary producers to worsen, i.e. for the prices of their exports to rise less than the prices of their imports. In other words, they have to export larger and larger *quantities* of primary products to earn sufficient to buy any given volume of imports.

The dice are loaded against primary producers in a more basic respect, too. Specializing in manufactures is likely to result in a faster rate of economic growth than concentrating on primary products. One of the main reasons for this is that the economies of large-scale production can be so much more easily achieved in manufacturing industry. Large-scale industrial enterprises – through a great variety of technical, managerial and marketing economies – can substantially cut their unit costs of production. Similar economies also exist in agriculture and extractive industries – but to a far lesser extent. And whereas it is comparatively easy for manufacturing firms to grow in size by take-overs and mergers, even the more limited potential economies of scale in agriculture are often not realized because the structure of agriculture – its geographical dispersion and larger numbers of producers – make it correspondingly difficult for increased concentration of production to take place.

But in addition to these 'static' economies of scale – the advantages of larger enterprises with given techniques and state of knowledge, there are 'dynamic' benefits which are enjoyed by giant corporations in manufacturing industry. The large firm is not only better able to exploit the existing state of know-how and techniques, it is also in the best position to add to that knowledge. Not only is it already technologically superior – it has the capability of enhancing that superiority still further. Competitiveness today often stems from success in developing new products and processes. This in turn depends on how much effort is channelled into research and development. This being an essentially hit-or-miss affair, the winners are usually those who spend most on it. Thus even if rich and poor countries devote the same proportion of their national resources to research and development, it is the rich which are most likely to hit the jackpots. In fact, poor countries can anyway generally afford only a smaller *proportion* of their resources to be used for these purposes. In 1980, for instance, underdeveloped countries accounted for a mere 6 per cent of world expenditure on research and development, according to UNESCO.

For all these reasons, then, the apparently 'liberal' system of free trade is heavily biased against underdeveloped countries. Freedom of trade, free competition, is only *fair* if the partners in the exercise are equal to begin with. Given an initial inequality the major beneficiaries will inevitably be the stronger partners – and although the weaker ones *may* incidentally benefit, the gap between them will continue to widen. None of this is to argue that underdeveloped countries should withdraw into attempted self-sufficiency. There are real gains from international trade which they would be foolish to forfeit. But what is questionable is whether *maximizing* trade is an appropriate policy if the policy objective is to bring about some narrowing of present international inequalities.

So much for the theory. What has happened in practice? The interwar years showed just how serious any substantial fall-off in international trade can be. Rich countries, facing major unemployment problems, tried to solve them by protectionist policies aimed at increasing the share of declining demand going to their own producers. But by cutting down on imports they reduced other countries' incomes – which then fed back in the form of higher unemployment in their own export industries. The enormous shrinkage in the volume of world trade which resulted from these self-defeating attempts to 'export' unemployment was a major factor in intensifying the world depression of those years.

When, therefore, the rich nations came together in the postwar period to discuss ways of avoiding a repetition of this catastrophe, their discussions centred on the need for liberalization of the world payments and trade system. Out of those discussions emerged three major international institutions – the International Monetary

Fund, the General Agreement on Tariffs and Trade, and the World Bank.

The IMF was designed to avoid the need for countries to resort to restrictive measures to deal with their balance of payments problems – by creating a pool of foreign exchange available for meeting short-term imbalances. GATT was to serve as a forum in which agreements could be negotiated for the progressive dismantling of barriers to trade – quota restrictions, exchange control and tariffs. And the World Bank was to channel investment resources more freely throughout the international economy.

None of these, at least in their pristine form, have worked wholly in the interests of the less developed three quarters of the world. Poor countries' balance of payments difficulties are generally chronic and structural – not temporary, so that the terms on which IMF assistance has been given have been quite inappropriate. The IMF 'medicine' of currency devaluation, cuts in public spending and lowering of import barriers has often made poverty worse for the majority of people in the borrowing countries. The World Bank operates essentially on commercial lines and has tended, for example, to promote large-scale growing of cash crops for export rather than small-scale food production for local consumption. And GATT, by demanding the *reciprocal* spread of tariff reductions, has moved further towards a system of world free trade, which as we have seen, works to the relative detriment of the weaker economies. The GATT has also, through the Multi-Fibre Arrangement, sanctioned increasing protectionism by industrial countries against imports of clothing and textiles from poor countries. On top of that the rich countries have further liberalized trade during the postwar period within regional groupings like the European Community.

One way of judging the effect of these various institutions and policies is to compare the international trading structure as it *would* be if its object was primarily one of assisting less developed countries and reducing international inequalities, to the actual state of affairs as it exists now.

If we were really concerned to help poor countries through the international trade mechanism, what system would have to be created? We would certainly not impose barriers against them selling to us. We would say 'export to us what you will, quite freely'.

But it would not do to expect reciprocally free entry into their markets as part of the bargain. Rich countries would have to agree that poor economies should be allowed to protect their infant industries on an appropriate scale. What is required, given the present degree of international economic inequality, is what Myrdal calls a 'dual standard'.[1] Rich countries would have to accept protectionist restrictions from poor countries which they themselves have agreed not to use.

Still more would be needed. Merely to allow free entry into rich countries of exports from poor countries would not be enough because such goods would still have to compete with the products of other advanced and technologically superior countries. What is therefore called for is not just free access to developed markets but preferential entry. If the object of the exercise is to narrow inequalities, then the poorer countries would have to enjoy 'positive discrimination'.

Furthermore, there would need to be correspondingly discriminatory policies with regard to international liquidity, the terms of trade and investment flows. A serious attempt to deal with development problems on an international scale would require measures aimed at stabilizing primary product prices at a high and increasing level, at linking increases in international liquidity to development needs, and at ensuring an adequate flow of multilateral aid.

The actual system of international trade is very different from this poor-country ideal. Take first the primary products on which they are largely dependent for foreign exchange earnings. We have already noted some of the difficulties associated with such dependence – that the demand for such commodities is likely to be slowly growing in relation to supply. Since, in addition to this, the supply and demand are, on the one hand, subject to wide fluctuations because of natural factors, and, on the other hand, are particularly susceptible to speculative pressures, the result is that primary product markets are generally characterized by extreme price instability. In principle, the problem is soluble through schemes for regulating the total production of such commodities, and by the international building-up of buffer stocks to even out

1. Myrdal, G., *Economic Theory and Underdeveloped Regions*, Duckworth, 1957.

variations in supply. In practice, however, there has been relatively little success along these lines. Partly this has been because of the reluctance of rich-country consumers of primary products to agree to schemes which are likely to raise the prices which they have to pay. Partly it is due to the difficulties of getting poor producers themselves to agree on output planning. What is in the interest of the group as a whole may conflict with that of particular members. Thus agreements by existing producers to restrict production in order to keep prices up will be opposed by new producers just entering the field. Such arrangements, moreover, are inherently unstable – as changing circumstances make it periodically profitable for particular members to break away and to pursue an independent course of action. And a final problem of stabilizing primary product prices at a high level stems from the fact that many primary products are produced in large quantities by the rich countries themselves. Schemes which other consumer countries might be prepared to accept as a means of helping poorer ones may seem rather less deserving of their support when some of the major beneficiaries are already very affluent.

The most dramatic and far-reaching example of producer countries acting together to raise the price of a raw material was in 1973, when OPEC quadrupled the price of oil. Against the background of the Arab Israeli War, OPEC managed to wrest control of both pricing and production rates from the multinational oil companies. It was the first time since the colonial era that a group of underdeveloped countries had acted in this way. Of course oil is a particularly valuable commodity without which the wheels of industry would literally grind to a halt and hardly any other group of commodity producers have been able to follow the OPEC example. One result of the cartel's action was to bring about a huge shift of wealth from the industrial nations to the oil exporters, although much of the extra money paid to OPEC was quite quickly deposited with the western banking system (as we shall see in the next section). Another effect was that oil users became interested in conserving petroleum and began to explore new sources for oil, such as the North Sea, which hitherto had been too costly to be worthwhile. In 1973 OPEC produced 56 per cent of world petroleum but by 1982 this had fallen to only 33 per cent. With the onset of the recession which began in 1979, OPEC found it increasingly difficult to maintain price levels. In 1980 world oil consumption was, in fact, 3 per cent *less* than it had been in 1973.

With regard to access to the markets of rich countries, many primary commodities are in fact allowed in duty free. This is not generally *concessionary*. When the primary products are non-competitive with their own output it is clearly in the interests of rich consumer countries to allow free entry. However, when primary products *are* competitive, the position is altogether more restrictive. In the case of the European Community, for example, grain and meat imports are subject to levies which raise the import price to the higher levels needed by economically inefficient domestic products. Before Britain joined the Community this was not so. Overseas producers were free to send their produce into the British market without restriction. This did not mean, however, that British farmers were unprotected; what happened was that after selling their output in open competition with low cost producers from outside, they were then paid 'deficiency payments' to bring their income up to an agreed level. In this way, the amount of food produced in Britain was kept much higher than it would have been without official support. There may or may not be good arguments in favour of such protection – from the British point of view. That is not at issue here. What is certain is that non-tariff support of primary producers in advanced countries restricts the market opportunities for exports from poorer countries. It should also be remembered that this is not just true of a group of products which can be produced only in temperate zones. Sugar beet, for instance, is an example of an artificially induced development of European agriculture which competes directly with small tropical producers. Under the Common Agricultural Policy the Community by 1982 was producing half as much sugar again as it could consume. Imports are limited to 1·3 million tonnes from underdeveloped countries and from being a net importer of sugar as late as 1973, the European Community is today the biggest single exporter of sugar on the world market. These exports have to be heavily subsidized as Community sugar beet prices are often two or three times the price of sugar cane grown in the Third World.

One final problem arising for primary products stems from the existence of regional groupings such as the European Community.

Six African, Caribbean and Pacific countries (known as the ACP states) are linked to the Community under the Lomé Convention. This aid and trade pact gives preferential access for some of their primary products within the Common Market countries. But the membership of such groups as this (as was the case with Commonwealth preference) generally depends on the countries' having previously had imperial links with the various metropolitan powers. What is implied in such preference is, therefore, a discrimination against other primary producers – the Lomé Convention includes only 12 per cent of the Third World's population. Moreover, the existence of regional groupings such as these, each with their system of special preferences, helps to splinter the poor primary producers into different interest groups and to make it difficult for them to present a united front against rich consumer countries.

The overall effect of rich-country international trade policies is therefore to add to, rather than counteract, the natural handicaps involved in over-concentration on primary production by the poorer nations; and when underdeveloped countries try to reduce that excessive dependence on a handful of primary commodities, they encounter still more severe trading problems.

A growing number of underdeveloped countries have understandably tried to escape from dependence on commodity trade by increasing their exports of manufactured goods, particularly textiles and clothing and more recently electronic equipment. These NICs of the Third World are characterized by low wage costs and rapidly expanding manufactured exports. But they are far from being a homogeneous group. Firstly, there are the small island economies, including Hong Kong, Taiwan and Singapore, which have spectacularly increased their wealth since the Second World War. Secondly, there are underdeveloped countries with sizeable manufacturing capacity for the home market and which also produce for export, such as India or Brazil. Thirdly, there are the much more agricultural countries, such as the Philippines and Sri Lanka, for example, where foreign companies are encouraged to set up production in 'free trade' or 'export processing zones' and are attracted by low wage rates, tax exemptions and no-strike agreements.

Manufactured goods or primary products which have been

processed to some degree are more overtly competitive with the output of developed countries, and formidable obstacles have been placed in the way of poorer nations increasing their exports of such goods. Rich countries generally have imposed tariffs on manufactures imported from less developed countries – tariffs which take the form of a sliding scale with the rate of duty increasing with the degree of processing. In other words, the more an under-developed country has been able to develop its own industrial capability, the greater the penalty which is imposed on it. Even more damaging in limiting the growth prospects of underdeveloped countries' exports are quota restrictions which many rich countries still apply – limiting the volume of manufactured imports which will be allowed in to a pre-arranged ceiling. Often, to avoid difficulties of securing GATT agreement to such restrictions, they are not *imposed* but instead take the form of 'voluntary agreements'. Poor countries have, of course, little option but to accept such arrangements since the alternative may well be that they are allowed to sell nothing at all.

Restrictions on imports of manufactures from low-cost countries commonly stem from the efforts of protectionist lobbies in rich countries which apply pressure on their governments not to allow domestic producers to go to the wall (with consequent increases in unemployment) as a result of competition from poor countries. Such competition, it is argued, is 'unfair'. Underdeveloped countries can undercut home producers only because they pay lower wages, and do not have the same social security burdens.

But if, as it might misleadingly seem from such arguments, the case for protection rests on anxiety about sweated labour in poor countries, then further restricting the markets in which underdeveloped countries can sell their goods is hardly likely to improve matters. And the interest of consumers, as opposed to producers, in developed countries is best served by allowing such imports in.

What stands in the way of rich countries adopting a more liberal attitude to low-cost manufactured imports, is partly the strength of pressure groups defending existing domestic producers – and partly the inflexibility of their economic systems. What *ought* to happen, in the textbook economy, is that resources in rich countries displaced by low-cost imports from outside will be diverted into other lines of production in which they can be more efficiently deployed – with improved productivity. In practice, however, as the British textile or coal industries illustrate, there are considerable difficulties in ensuring that capital and labour displaced by foreign competition are quickly redeployed in more useful directions.

These are real difficulties which must be taken into account in the timing of trade liberalization. However, imports from the NICs are only one reason for the large-scale loss of jobs in traditional manufacturing areas in the industrial countries. Much more significant have been the recession which began in 1979, increased productivity and competition between industrial countries. To some extent the NICs have been used as a scapegoat for more fundamental industrial and employment problems in the richer countries. It is still a good deal easier for mature economies to overcome problems caused by immobility of resources than it is for underdeveloped countries to develop through diversification in face of continued restrictions on their export sales by a handful of much richer countries.

To sum up, then, the actual practice of rich countries in international trade is basically the reverse of what ought to be happening if it were the development of poorer countries which was primarily at stake. In fact, what developed countries say to the less developed is broadly along these lines: 'If you care to export to us primary commodities which we need and which we do not produce ourselves, then please feel free to do so. We shall put no barrier in your way and your only problem will be those arising from price instability and a relatively slowly growing demand (partly caused by our capability and interest in producing synthetic substitutes) – which means that you will probably have to export larger and larger quantities to pay for any given volume of imports of our manufactures. You can't, of course, expect us to be quite so liberal with regard to those primary products which we can, if only by offering subsidies, sometimes produce ourselves. If, however, you decide to hedge against these difficulties by processing yourselves some of the raw materials which would otherwise have been sent to us, then we're afraid that some disincentive is called for. Duty will be payable on such imports. And just to make the point quite plain, the going gets tougher: the more the processing which you undertake, the higher the rate of duty. And if one of the ways in which you try to break out of the vicious circle of underdevelopment is by diversifying into manufacturing final goods, then either we will nullify your possible comparative advantage by very high tariffs, or we will arrange matters so that the volume of exports you achieve is too small to worry us.'

What *is* the answer for poor countries? How can the rich countries ever be persuaded to match their pious sentiments by helpful action in the sphere of international trade? One of the main contributory causes of poor-country difficulties is the weakness of their bargaining position with richer members of the international economy. Developed countries, for one thing, are themselves primary producers – with, as has already been noted, the increasing capability both to economize in the use of natural commodities and to produce synthetic substitutes. Moreover, it is relatively easy for a handful of rich countries to present a united front in negotiation with a large number of small and often desperately anxious small producers.

There is an analogy here with the development of trade unionism within advanced economies. Under the Combination Acts in Britain, for example, associations of workers were banned – on the argument that fair competition demanded that each employee should be free to strike his own individual wage bargain with the employer. This notion of 'fairness' bears a strong family resemblance to the liberalism of free trade. In both cases it is illusory. Free bargaining between individual workers and employers would only be fair if they were of equal strength – which they are not. The employer clearly has the whip hand because he has more reserves to fall back on and a wider range of options in the use of his resources.

Equity in this case was only achieved by the introduction of collective bargaining – the acceptance of the right of workers to form themselves into trade unions and through concerted action to face the employers over the negotiating table on an equal basis.

This, in the end, may prove to be the solution for poor countries too. Individually their relationships with rich countries are bound to be highly unequal. Concessions can be wrung from the developed economies only when the poor speak with a single voice. And this indeed is what was tried during the sixties.

In 1964 the United Nations Conference on Trade and Development (UNCTAD) took place in Geneva. At this conference, the poorer nations, the Seventy-Five as they were then known, for the first time collectively expressed their view that existing international trade arrangements represented a major obstacle to their drive towards development. They viewed GATT as essentially a 'rich man's club'. What was needed, they argued, was a drastic revision of the world trading structure broadly along the lines which we have already discussed. To this end UNCTAD became a permanent institution with its own Secretary-General and Secretariat – to function as a research and pressure group serving the interests of the poorer two thirds.

So far at least its successes have been very limited. At subsequent UNCTAD sessions (New Delhi 1968, Santiago 1972, Nairobi 1976, Manila 1979 and Belgrade 1983), developed countries proved readier to agree in principle to the lines of reform suggested by poor countries than to get down to the business of discussing the way in which they could be effectively implemented. Thus a General Scheme of Preferences for exports from underdeveloped countries was adopted to give freer access to markets in the rich world. This is non-reciprocal (i.e. the developing countries are not expected to reduce their own tariffs in return), but many sensitive items, such as textiles, are excluded from the scheme as implemented by the industrial countries. A Common Fund to help finance the stabilization of commodity prices, first accepted in principle by UNCTAD in 1976, was still not operational by 1985. Indeed, the recession brought about a collapse in commodity prices, which fell by a third between 1980 and 1982.

Why has it proved so difficult to reform the international trade system on a more equitable basis? Much of the blame can be laid at the door of the developed countries. The existence of UNCTAD has at least been successful in revealing the very limited extent to which rich countries are at present prepared to move. Their reluctance to make more than minimal concessions can at worst be interpreted as evidence that they recognize that the present system works very much in their own favour – and that they never had any real intention of abandoning that privileged position. At best it could be argued that the time for reform has been an unpropitious one for the governments of developed countries. The fall in the price of oil in 'real' terms, that is taking account of inflation, in the late 1970s and in actual cash terms in the early

1980s, undermined much of the bargaining power of the Third World countries (now known as the Group of 77). The industrial countries were immediately concerned about their own balance of payments and inflation problems; later on the recession made the industrial nations even less willing to make any 'concessions' to the underdeveloped countries. There were always pressing reasons for postponing any action.

These arguments apply *a fortiori* to the United States, and the trouble is that other developed countries more willing to move along the lines demanded by UNCTAD have been reluctant to do so unilaterally. They wait on general agreement. Why, they ask, should *they* offer concessions when the richest country in the world is unprepared to do so?

The other problem of UNCTAD has been splits between the less developed countries themselves. Their apparent solidarity at the inception of UNCTAD was short-lived. Their common concern has been overshadowed by conflicting interests. Their general demands have, as a result, been more moderate than might have been expected, and it has continued to be possible for developed countries to buy them off individually rather than have to face concerted collective bargaining strength. Some of the better-off oil exporters have begun to feel they have more in common with the industrial nations than with the poorer underdeveloped nations.

Supposing, however, that developed countries *were* to practise what they preach and that the international trade system were reorganized on terms more favourable to poor countries. How important a contribution could that make to their development? Why, in fact, is increasing trade significant for them?

Increased international trade is vital to their development effort in two main respects. Firstly, it is the source of foreign exchange earnings. These are required for imports of goods from advanced economies which are needed to overcome particular development bottlenecks. They are also needed to service the mounting volume of foreign debt with which poor countries are now encumbered. It is this which highlights the absurdity of rich countries' illiberal attitude towards imports from low-cost poor producers. They make loans to them – and then create obstacles to them earning the wherewithal for their repayment.

Trade is also important for poor countries as a supplement to inadequate domestic markets. In Africa, in particular, fragmentation has proceeded to the point at which most states have only tiny markets quite incapable of supporting any range of modern industries. For them, foreign trade is essential if their embryo industries are to begin to achieve economies of scale necessary for competitiveness.

It is this consideration which is the most powerful argument for further regional groupings of poor countries in economic communities. A number of such groupings already exist – in west and southern Africa and the Caribbean, for example. The problems involved in such communities are, however, substantial.

It is not sufficient for a group of countries merely to come together to form a free trade area. Certainly the total market will increase as a result. But, as we have already seen, free trade tends to work to the greater benefit of rich partners in the enterprise than the poor ones. Thus it will be the more-developed poor country which gains more than the less-developed poor country from schemes of regional co-operation.

This can be overcome only by positive planning policies to ensure that investment resources are allocated on an equitable basis between the different members – planning which views the siting of new projects from the point of view of the group as a whole. But what this boils down to is taxing members of one country for the benefit of members of another, i.e. creating an economic community rather than a mere free trade area. Acceptance of these implications, however, requires a common identity of interest in the community as a whole – the development of a supra-national consciousness. Whether economic integration can precede political unification is highly questionable – and for all the talk of Pan-Africanism, for example, steps towards greater integration are bound to be hesitant in a continent of states which have only recently acquired political independence from imperial rule. Measures for increasing trade flows between developing countries therefore pose not dissimilar difficulties to those arising with rich country/poor country trading relationships.

There is a further reason for doubting whether international trade can today act as an engine for the transmission of economic development as it did during the nineteenth century. Even with free

or preferential access to developed markets how successful can
poor countries hope to be in selling them manufactures? A major
'take-off' export industry in earlier periods was textiles – particularly appropriate for this role because of the availability of raw
material, its relative labour-intensity and the comparatively simple
techniques involved. But this is no longer the case. Cheap cotton
shirts from Pakistan or Hong Kong have a limited appeal in, for
example, the British market where they face competition from
much more technologically sophisticated man-made materials –
with their drip-dry, minimum-iron advantages. This 'taste-gap'
paralleling the technological gap between rich and poor countries
has made it increasingly difficult for poor countries, who now have
to import sophisticated machinery and rayon if they are to produce
goods acceptable to consumers in more developed parts of the
world. Furthermore, it has been suggested that the micro-chip
technological revolution may make it more economical once again
to manufacture products in the industrial nations and take away
the 'natural' advantage of cheap labour in the underdeveloped
countries. Already 'outward processing' has become quite common, where a company based in an industrial nation takes a
product through various stages of manufacture and only the most
labour intensive are sited in the Third World.

All in all, the trade prospects for poor countries are gloomy; and
rich countries are prepared to do little to help. Underdeveloped
countries are forced into severe competition with each other for
limited trade outlets. And their difficulty in finding suitable export
goods to replace their present unhealthy reliance on a few primary
products emphasizes once again the problem of development in a
world already sharply divided by generations of economic and
technological inequality.

2. Giving and receiving aid

*Receiving aid is ... like making love to an elephant. There is no
pleasure in it, you run the risk of being crushed and it takes years
before you see the results.*[2]

2. Streeten, P., 'A Poor Nation's Guide to Getting Aid'. This article first appeared
in *New Society*, 1 February, 1968.

Trade, as we have just seen, is weighted against underdeveloped countries. But the commercial exchange of goods is only one element in the relationship between rich and poor countries. In addition, there has also been a substantial flow of resources – capital, labour, information, skills and food. These are commonly grouped together under the heading of 'aid'. The nature of the aid relationship is highly contentious and a vast amount of literature has been produced on every aspect of the subject. How much aid should the developed nations be providing, what form should it take, and how effective has it been? What, for that matter, *is* aid and what is the purpose of the aid operation? What are the motivations of donors in offering aid and of recipients in accepting it? Who should be responsible for disbursing it and on what criteria should it be distributed? Very different answers have been given to these questions. In this section we shall look at some of the broad issues which have arisen about aid-giving within the present framework, and then return to the subject again in Part Five to consider how that framework might be reformulated.

Although aid is a highly controversial topic, some interesting consensuses of opinion have developed in recent years which equally call for explanation.

(i) There is, first of all, a growing disillusionment with aid – on the part of both donors and recipients. Earlier optimism about the effectiveness of aid has now somewhat evaporated. In rich countries, taxpayers and their elected representatives have increasingly questioned the value of aid in buying political support or promoting their own economic interests. At the same time, poor countries have become more fearful of the threat to their independence which aid has often seemed to represent. Aid is not always politically popular in practice although in principle it seems to have become more acceptable in some parts of the rich world. For example, a Gallup poll in 1983 found 59 per cent of the British population in favour of their country giving help to poorer countries, and a European Community survey a year later claimed 82 per cent of the public in the member states in favour of aid for the Third World.

(ii) Particularly in the rich countries, there is another odd alliance of views in that the Anti-Aid school comprises economists at opposite ends of the political spectrum. It is those of the extremer

Right and those of the extremer Left who most fundamentally
question the role of aid in promoting economic development. They
do so from very different standpoints and use quite different
arguments, but there is a common core of agreement between them
that development, if it is to be genuine and sustained, must be an
essentially indigenous process.

However, before discussing some of the basic controversies
which surround the issue, something should firstly be said about
the origin of the aid relationship – and also about what *constitutes*
aid.

The notion that rich countries could, and should, assist poorer
nations in their development efforts is essentially a postwar one.
In the decade after 1945, there were four major factors at work
directing advanced economies towards embarking on hopeful
programmes of foreign aid.

(i) This was, first of all, the period in which a large number of
countries achieved political independence. Poverty and international inequality, which to some extent had been hidden by the
colonial relationship, now became problems which it was the
openly avowed aim of every emergent state to solve. Both the
former imperial powers and those which had no such colonial
background were forced into an awareness of these problems and
accepted, in differing degrees, a common responsibility for their
solution. Partly, this assumption of responsibility was an international parallel of the heightened social consciousness which,
within rich countries, was pushing policy into 'welfare state' directions.

(ii) Aid was further seen, in the immediate postwar years, as a
major weapon in winning the Cold War. Within the new alignment
of world power, rapid economic progress of the less developed
countries was viewed as a bulwark against the further spread of
Communism.

(iii) Advances in economics also had a part to play. Developed
economies during the thirties had themselves faced major economic
crises in the form of massive cyclical unemployment – a challenge
to their affluence which had been overcome by a breakthrough in
economic understanding: the Keynesian 'revolution' had shown
how management of the level of aggregate demand – through
monetary and fiscal policies – could eliminate the worst excesses of

the business cycle. With that problem basically solved, economists returned to a much earlier preoccupation – of how, not merely to stabilize economies at a high level of employment, but also to achieve steady economic *growth*. Flushed by their earlier success, they did so in the confidence that economic matters *were* amenable to rational ordering. It was not long before the products of this new interest in growth economics were being applied to the far more pressing situations of poor countries, and a growing volume of literature on 'development economics' began to appear.

(iv) And, finally, as proof of the pudding, there was the case study provided by what was at the time going on in Western Europe itself. Germany, for example, had by the end of the war been reduced to a condition ostensibly similar to the more chronic poverty of underdeveloped countries. Incomes had fallen to rock bottom. The productive capacity of the economy had been destroyed. The factories, machines, roads and railways needed to produce goods had been largely devastated; and yet, through Marshall Aid – the injection of American capital on a massive scale – Germany was rapidly restored to economic health. It had worked for Europe, so why couldn't a similar exercise be mounted to stimulate the economic development of the poorer parts of the world?

It was against this background that large-scale aid programmes developed, with the total net flow of resources from non-Communist developed countries and multilateral agencies to underdeveloped countries reaching no less than 61·8 billion US dollars in 1983.

19. Net flow of resources to underdeveloped countries (billions US dollars)					
	1960	1970	1975	1979	1983*
Official	4·6	7·0	13·8	22·8	27·5
Private	3·1	7·0	25·7	47·7	34·3

* estimated figures

Sources: World Bank, *World Development Report 1984*, OUP, 1985, & OECD Statistics.

After the 1973 oil price rise the newly rich oil exporting countries deposited their 'surplus' petro-dollars in western banks. By 1975, as the table shows, the banks were then lending this money in huge quantities to the underdeveloped countries. Private lending fell sharply in 1980 with the onset of the recession but it recovered later, to some extent, as the banks found themselves forced to make new loans so that the poor nations would be able to continue paying interest on their earlier borrowings.

Although the total flow of resources to the underdeveloped countries – 61·8 billion US dollars – *is* a large sum, it is worth relating it to another large number. In 1983 over 600 billion US dollars were devoted to military expenditure worldwide. As Herr Willy Brandt, the former West German Chancellor, pointed out in his introduction to the Brandt Report[3], *official* development aid amounts to less than 5 per cent of annual arms spending.

Anyway, a number of qualifications have to be made to these crude figures before they can be used as an index of mounting development assistance from the rich countries. In the first place, the *rate of increase* in the flow of resources from developed to underdeveloped economies takes no account of its value in real terms. Official aid has actually fallen in value between the 1960s and the 1980s. Private flows were also in real terms not significantly greater in 1983 than in 1960. For most of this period, moreover, the rich countries were growing increasingly affluent year by year. But in the case of nearly every major aid donor, their aid contribution, as a percentage of their national income, markedly declined. What is more, the figures we have been considering so far are of the *total* flow of resources from rich to poor countries. These are, in fact, an aggregate of two broad categories: firstly, official assistance consisting of funds made available by governments on a concessional basis, and secondly, flows of private foreign investment. The increased total flow during the seventies was due to a rapid expansion of *private* investment, with official assistance falling by the early eighties even in money terms.

Further, the following table shows how small official development assistance has been in relation to donor countries' gross national products.

3. *North–South: A Programme for Survival*, report of the Independent Commission on International Development Issues, Pan, 1980.

20. Official development assistance flows (billions US dollars)					
	1960	1970	1975	1980	1982	1983*
OECD	4·6	7·0	13·8	27·3	27·8	27·5*
OPEC	nil	nil	6·2	9·7	6·8*	n.a.
Total	4·6	7·0	20·0	37·0	34·6	

*estimated figures

Source: World Bank, op. cit.

21. Official development assistance as % of GNP (1982)				
OECD			OPEC	
Italy	0·24	France	0·75	Nigeria	0·08
New Zealand	0·28	West Germany	0·48	Algeria	0·29
UK	0·37	Denmark	0·77	Venezuela	0·32
Austria	0·53	USA	0·27	Libya	0·18
Japan	0·29	Sweden	1·02	Saudi Arabia	2·82
Belgium	0·60	Norway	0·99	Kuwait	4·86
Finland	0·30	Switzerland	0·25	United Arab Emirates	2·06
Netherlands	1·08			Qatar	3·80
Australia	0·57				
Canada	0·42	Total OECD	0·38	Total OPEC	1·22
				Total centrally planned economies	0·14

Source: ibid. and Overseas Development Administration, London.

But can private foreign investment conceivably be included as 'aid'? How in fact should aid be defined? It is surely highly misleading to include purely commercial transactions. If investors in a rich country decide to set up a business in a poor country, they do so in the belief that it will show a satisfactory rate of return. It *may* be that development of the poorer country is stimulated (though see Part Five, section 3), but that is incidental. However, to classify such a transaction as 'aid' – with its connotation of self-sacrificing charity is, as Myrdal has called it, mere 'opportunistic juggling' of the statistics. If we are to use the term at all, then it is only right to reserve it for those flows which take place on a concessional basis – with the donor accepting a lower than commercial return. If I borrow £1,000 from the bank at the going rate, to be repaid over three years, I have no particular feeling of gratitude. A gift of £1,000 is a very different matter, as also is a loan at 3 per cent, or one which can be repaid over 50 years. The first is wholly 'aid', the others partially so to the extent that the terms are easier than the commercial rate.

There are two other qualifications to be made in determining the part of the total flow of resources which should be classed as aid. If you lend me a sum of money at concessional rates but insist that it should be spent in your own shop where prices happen to be 10 per cent higher than elsewhere, then the value of the loan to me is correspondingly reduced. 'Tied' aid of this kind has been extremely common. And, secondly, not all 'aid' is necessarily for promoting economic development. It may take the form of military hardware or political subventions to princely rulers.

By the time that all these qualifications have been taken into account, the remaining flow of resources from rich countries to poor countries, on concessional terms, for the purpose of promoting economic development, looks a great deal less impressive than the overall total.

But that is not the end of the matter. There is a flow in the other direction – from poor to rich – which has to be offset against the aid total before the *net* contribution from developed countries can be finally calculated. The three main elements in this 'reverse flow' are the payment of interest on past private and official loans – which is now amounting, in the case of many developing countries, to an alarming proportion of their foreign exchange earnings; the outflow of repatriated profits on private investments; and the loss of human capital involved in the brain-drain of skilled personnel from poor countries to rich countries.

All of these are serious problems, but the most damaging in the 1980s is the debt crisis, which, in the words of a Commonwealth Group of Experts, means 'The world's financial safety is balanced on a knife edge'.[4] By 1984 underdeveloped countries owed 810 billion US dollars to the industrial nations, 350 billion of which

4. *The Debt Crisis and the World Economy*, report by a Commonwealth Group of Experts, July 1984, Commonwealth Secretariat, Marlborough House, London SW1.

were owing from Latin America. In the 1970s the western banks were only too anxious to lend their petro-dollars to the underdeveloped countries, particularly to the better-off nations. Interest rates were not burdensome, the world economy was growing, official aid was not as readily available as it had been in the 1960s and there seemed every prospect that the underdeveloped nations would be able to repay. However by the end of the decade interest rates were very high, a recession was beginning and many of the loans were becoming due for repayment. For some of the acutely indebted countries, interest payments alone absorbed between one third and one half of their export earnings. In the summer of 1982 Mexico, a middle income underdeveloped country and an oil exporter, threatened to default on its repayments.

The underdeveloped nations complain that the world recession with its associated fall in commodity prices and increased protectionism against manufactures exported from the Third World, is not of their making. They argue that the slump has been made worse by the deflationary policies pursued by the western nations. Nor do the underdeveloped nations feel they have any control over interest rates. Every one per cent rise in interest rates in the United States added another 3 billion US dollars to the debt of the underdeveloped countries in 1984. The concern of the banks has been to maintain the flow of interest payments at all costs, which they have done by making new loans or 'rolling over' the dates by which repayments are due. They have also generally refused to re-schedule debts until the underdeveloped country has reached agreement with the IMF on new loan facilities. This IMF 'stamp of approval' is only available if the debtor nation is prepared to implement various deflationary policies, the aim of which is to increase export earnings and thus the country's ability to make interest payments and repay its debts. The IMF package of devaluation, cuts in government spending and dismantling of protective import barriers, also has the effect of making the underdeveloped country poorer – at least in the short run. It is argued that the deflationary policies imposed on so many underdeveloped countries all at once, have deepened the recession and made it less likely that the private banks will ever get their money back.

Even the potential benefits of an increasing flow of *technical* assistance to underdeveloped countries (now amounting to over

20 per cent of total official aid) have been offset by migration from poor to rich countries. Since a shortage of specific skills characterizes poor economies, the provision of expertise and training programmes could clearly play an important part in promoting development. In practice, however, such assistance has often been ill-adapted to local needs: it has embodied techniques relevant to the quite different conditions of capital-rich economies. Moreover, it has frequently imposed absurd burdens on the recipient countries which have been expected to supplement the salaries of expatriate staff and to provide them with expensive housing, transport and other ancillary facilities. And finally, a sizeable proportion of technical assistance has taken the form of providing student training in the donor countries: the number of such students who then opt to stay abroad permanently is one element in the mounting loss of skilled personnel currently experienced by the underdeveloped world. Although the evidence is not available to come to any precise conclusion, earlier estimates suggested, for example, that 'for the US, immigration almost certainly represents a more substantial flow of human capital than does technical assistance in the reverse direction, and that for the UK the balance is possibly also in the UK's favour, though to a much smaller extent'.[5]

It is possible that the overall reverse flow has now reached such proportions that it is the poor countries who have sometimes been 'aiding' the rich. Myrdal quotes US Senator Charles McC. Mathias, Jr, to the effect that 'Capital flows *from* Latin America and *into* the United States are now over four times as great as the flow south. The countries of Latin America in a way are actually giving foreign aid to the United States, the wealthiest country in the world.'[6] More recently, the President of the World Bank, Mr A. W. 'Tom' Clausen, stated in 1984 that the underdeveloped countries 'are paying back more to the banks than the banks are lending'. The Amex Bank review in the same year calculated that the poor countries as a whole paid back to the banks in 1983 some 11 billion US dollars more than they received in new loans.

Certainly the aid record is far less praiseworthy than the official

5. Clifford and Osmond, World Development Handbook, C. Knight for Overseas Development Institute, 1971.

6. Quoted in Myrdal, G., *The Challenge of World Poverty*, Allen Lane The Penguin Press, 1970.

totals suggest. But before concluding that there is an urgent need for the volume of aid to be stepped up, we ought firstly to ask what is the purpose of aid? Can it make a genuine contribution to development? Is it necessary at all?

Why aid?

Aid defined on a concessional basis implies a conscious attempt on the part of governments in developed countries to generate a flow of resources to poorer countries which would not otherwise have taken place. Acceptance of the need for governments to intervene along these lines and deliberately to encourage movements of resources is a postwar phenomenon marking a break from traditional thinking on international economics. For traditional economists would argue that natural forces already worked to promote development and narrow economic inequalities between nations.

Rich countries, they would say, are characterized by an abundance of capital – on which the return is therefore relatively low. Labour, in such countries, on the other hand, tends to be expensive. In poor countries, the situation is the opposite – capital is in short supply, but there is plentiful cheap labour. In an unimpeded market system, two sets of forces will be set in motion.

Capital will tend to flow from rich countries to poor countries, seeking a higher rate of return and combining with the cheap labour available there. Labour, on the other hand, will move in the reverse direction. With perfect mobility of both capital and labour, incomes in the two countries would eventually be equalized. Admittedly, perfect mobility does not exist, but such flows of factors which do take place will have an equalizing effect.

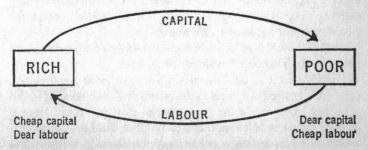

Unfortunately, this classical picture is wildly remote from reality.

Private capital goes where private investors think they can make money. And that is seldom in underdeveloped countries. Certainly labour is cheap there – but it is generally the wrong type of labour – unskilled, undisciplined, unused to modern techniques. Moreover, other aspects of underdevelopment – soft administration, interventionist economic policies, political instability – represent precisely that climate of uncertainty which is anathema to private investment. 'Success breeds success' is the motto for private capital. It concentrates in regions where 'external economies' are evident – availability of skilled labour, appropriate transport and communications, closeness to markets. It is difficult enough, within rich countries, to disperse investment to less prosperous regions. Substantial inducements have to be offered to persuade firms to locate new plants in the relatively depressed areas of Britain. Such difficulties are compounded when it is a question of capital moving between countries at different levels of economic development. Indeed, far from capital moving on a large scale from rich to poor countries, it would flow in the opposite direction were it not for barriers to the export of capital imposed by the governments of poor countries. (Although, since these are often rather ineffective, a substantial flight of capital *does* take place.)

Labour, of course, is inherently less mobile internationally than capital. Therefore, little equalizing effect can be expected from movements of workers from poor countries to richer ones. Natural immobility is reinforced by restrictive immigration policies on the part of the advanced countries. But to the extent that labour does move from less prosperous to more affluent countries, *which* labour is it? It is of those workers with initiative, those who are young enough to contemplate such an upheaval, those with the necessary skills to make it worthwhile – those workers, indeed, which the poorer country can least afford to lose.

The traditional view of likely capital and labour movements and their effects thus needs drastically revising.

To the extent that such movements do take place, the flows are perverse – leading not to an equalization of world incomes but to a further widening of the gap between rich and poor. Here is Myrdal's process of 'circular and cumulative causation' at work – with factor flow serving to further impoverish poor countries and benefit the rich.

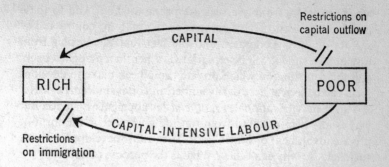

The point is that the labour which does move from poor to rich countries is generally 'capital-intensive' labour, that on which considerable resources have been invested through education and training. The loss in social terms to the poor country often greatly exceeds the gain to rich countries. The fact that British hospitals are staffed to their present degree by Indian doctors and West Indian nurses may represent only a marginal gain for the British economy. But the cost of training such personnel, measured by output forgone in their home countries, may be very substantial. From the point of view of the poorer countries, there might well be good reasons for restricting such immigration.

Again, despite what has been said, private capital *does* flow from rich countries to poor countries. But into which sectors? And to which countries? It goes where the return is substantial and relatively secure. A major attraction will be extractive industries – petroleum and mineral resources – which are capital-intensive, cater for external markets, and where dependence on unreliable indigenous resources is minimized. The snag, from the developing countries' point of view is that such 'enclave' activity may do little to stimulate local development since the *spread* effects of such investment are minimal. Then again, it will be those countries which offer the greatest prospect of political and social stability, and the most favourable concessionary terms, which will be chiefly successful in attracting foreign private investment. But, as has already been pointed out, development is a process demanding fundamental structural changes in attitudes and institutions. The very conditions most likely to stimulate development are those which investors from overseas are prone to shun. Add to these problems the fears of developing countries of losing control of key sectors of their economies, and the fact that the surplus from foreign investment will be repatriated rather than ploughed back, and the contribution which private capital can make to development can be seen as necessarily limited and often, indeed, negative.

This then is the rationale for *official* development assistance. But why is any help required from outside – whether in the form of private investment or official aid? After all *we* developed without such help, so why can't they? What is the purpose of aid?

The purpose of aid

There are three broad functions which it can be argued aid might serve: firstly, as an external supplement to inadequate domestic capital formation; secondly, as a means of overcoming foreign exchange constraints on economic development; and thirdly, as an agent for internationally diffusing economic and technical knowledge.

The three are not mutually exclusive. They may well overlap. But to some extent emphases on one or other roles of aid reflect different views of the development mechanism and the relative importance of possible blockages.

Supporters of aid most commonly see it in the first of these three roles. Certainly, it was on this basis that aid programmes were initiated in the postwar years. As has already been noted, two of the factors behind the novel idea that rich countries might assist poor ones through official capital flows were the apparent success of such measures in rehabilitating devastated Western Europe – and the hypotheses which were emerging from the new interest shown in the field of growth economics.

In analysing the nature of economic growth in developed countries, economists initially tended to exaggerate the role of capital accumulation. This over-simplified approach applied to underdeveloped economies suggested that their problems stemmed from inadequate savings due to low incomes. The savings-centred theory of development, stressing the need to make sacrifices in current consumption in order to achieve greater plough-back, is one which we have already criticized in Part Three, section 3. Certainly capital *is* an important factor in the development process. But without the necessary co-operant factors of know-how, skills, work discipline, entrepreneurship and general development-orientation, simply injecting capital into a poor economy is unlikely to put it on to a development course.

Then again, the view that foreign aid is necessary to supplement domestic savings is derived from the view that poor countries are unable to jack up savings ratios because of their low *per capita* incomes. It ignores the fact that they are also typified by extreme income inequality – so that substantial potential savings *can* be mobilized from the higher income groups, given the political will to do so. Indeed, *if* insufficient savings were the crux of the problem – if the development problem were simply one of raising savings 'from, say 5 per cent to 10 per cent' – then one would expect the development record of poorer countries to be rather more impressive than it is. For they have been very successful in increasing the proportions of their national products channelled into savings and investment. The Pearson Report described it as 'a dramatic achievement ... despite a common impression that poor countries are too poor to save anything, they have in fact mobilized the bulk of their investment capital'[7]. Except in low income Africa, domestic savings finance the bulk of total investment.

Finally, there is the question of how far it is possible to supplement domestic savings successfully from external sources. Three points need stressing in this respect:

(i) There is a real danger that availability of funds from external sources will dampen down the internal inducement to save. Aid may serve not to supplement domestic savings but as an excuse for failing to mobilize the domestic savings potential.

(ii) Foreign capital naturally tends to embody the techniques currently deployed in developed countries – technologically sophisticated and capital-intensive. In terms of the simple growth model, in other words, the increase in capital may be offset by a rise in the capital–output ratio. Moreover, since, as has already been argued, such techniques may be markedly inappropriate to the conditions of underdeveloped countries, they are likely to be used inefficiently – still further raising the capital–output ratio.

7. Pearson, *Partners in Development*, report of the Commission on International Development, Pall Mall Press, 1970, p. 31.

(iii) Much foreign capital – when it takes the form of private investment – tends, as we have seen, to be channelled into 'enclaves' such as mineral exploitation – with consequently little in the way of beneficial 'spread' effects to stimulate indigenous development.

22. Savings and investment as % of GNP 1981		
	Savings	*Investment*
Developing countries	23·2	27·0
Low income Asia	23·8	25·8
Low income Africa	5·9	16·6
Middle income oil importers	20·8	25·3
Middle income oil exporters	27·9	31·4

Source: World Bank, op. cit.

To sum up. The experience of two decades of wrestling with development problems has cast serious doubts on whether a shortage of capital is *the* crucial constraint in most poor countries. In some countries, it *is* clearly more important than in others. But even in these cases it is vital to ensure that receipt of aid is not used to mask the need for positive policies to mobilize domestic savings, or for implementation of painful but essential structural reform. And it is equally imperative, if aid is to be effective, that it should take the right form, embody appropriate techniques and be directed into those sectors dictated by development requirements rather than external interests.

These qualitative aspects of external assistance are as important as the total volume. But with regard to volume, it is perhaps worth remembering that in the case of postwar Germany, already referred to, injection of Marshall Aid capital took place on a gigantic scale. Aid per capita in this case greatly exceeded that which has flowed to most developing countries. It is interesting to speculate about the possible effects of aid on present underdeveloped countries if it were to be stepped up to correspondingly high per capita levels. The examples of Taiwan and South Korea suggest that a policy of 'overkill' in capital injection *can*, despite the qualifications already made, do the trick – if growth is the desired goal. Pouring in capital on an enormous scale, regardless of how much is wasted, may well in the end bring about faster economic growth – though these examples suggest that the price can be a loss of cultural identity.

A quite different rationale for aid-giving is one which stresses that a major bottleneck in economic development has been shortage of foreign exchange. Poor countries, being largely dependent on primary product exports and facing obstacles in developing manufactured exports, often encounter balance of payments problems – difficulties in earning enough foreign exchange to meet debt repayment obligations and to pay for necessary imports. This is not to argue that underdeveloped countries should be heavily reliant on imports. But imports can sometimes be a short-cut in the development process: inability to produce some strategic component for a manufacturing process may hold up a whole chain of developments. If the role of foreign exchange is pivotal in this respect then aid can help. Once again, its volume may be less important than its form. What is essentially required is 'free' foreign exchange – untied to either specific projects or to purchasing of specific goods from particular donors. And it is precisely this type of aid which is most often in short supply.

Finally, aid may be seen as a means of diffusing international techniques and know-how. It may take the form, not of goods or foreign exchange, but of technical assistance. Undoubtedly this may be of potentially great value to developing countries, enabling them to nurture skills and attitudes in short supply – thus making it possible for them to deploy limited capital resources more effectively. Historically, as was pointed out in the opening section, Japan was a prime example of extensively using foreign expertise in order to stimulate development-orientation. Once again, however, it is crucial that technical assistance introduces the *appropriate* techniques and that attitudes are changed in a way conducive to growth rather than biased against it. Too often this has not been the case. Personnel from developing countries have been taken abroad for technical training and acquired skills which are inapplicable to their domestic situation; worse still, they may imbibe western attitudes which make them contemptuous of the homespun process by which development takes place. Moreover, attempts to construct a 'technological balance of payments' suggest that the

international exchange of information and technical expertise
continues to be largely between already developed countries. Western Europe and Japan are far more important beneficiaries of
research and development in the more advanced countries than are
the underdeveloped economies.

In view of the fact that the present forms of aid seem ill-designed
to serve *any* of its potential roles, it is not surprising that so much
scepticism has arisen about the value of aid as an instrument to
promote economic development. What *is* surprising is that those
who criticize the aid process most severely do so from very different
political premises.

Aid: a view from the Right

Professor Lord Bauer of the London School of Economics is
perhaps the most extreme critic, and he has asserted for many years
'that the best policy would be a complete termination of the aid
programme'.[8] His view is that 'foreign aid can do little or nothing
for development or the relief of poverty'. He believes 'It is also
questionable whether people in the West should be taxed for the
benefit of the governments of societies where people refuse to kill
animals, as in India, or let women take paid work, as in many
Moslem countries.'[9]

Bauer argues that aid is not at all central to development. After
all 'Large-scale development occurs in many places without foreign
aid, and did so long before foreign aid was invented.' For him,
'economic achievement depends on the conduct of people and their
governments' and not on overseas aid. 'It diminishes the people of
the Third World to suggest that, although they crave for material
progress, unlike the West they cannot achieve it without external
doles,' he contends. Bauer argues that if it is shortage of capital
which is the missing link, aid is unnecessary, 'because governments
and enterprises in the Third World which can use capital pro-
ductively can borrow commercially at home and abroad'. If it is
not capital which is the bottleneck, then aid is bound to be
ineffective anyway.

8. Bauer, P., House of Commons Select Committee on Overseas Aid, Minutes
of Evidence Sub-Committee A, Session 1969–70, HMSO, pp. 203–25.

9. Bauer, P., *Reality and Rhetoric*, Weidenfeld and Nicolson, London, 1984.
Further quotes appearing in this section are from this source.

Moreover, there are, according to Bauer, a number of deleterious side-effects of the aid process. Firstly, it increases 'the resources and power of recipient governments compared with the rest of society'. Secondly, it enables those governments 'to pursue even extremely damaging policies for years on end because the inflow of funds conceals from the population at least temporarily some of the worst effects of their policies'. Thirdly, it makes developing countries more dependent on the West and is likely to turn the poor into 'paupers', so that aid grants have to be continued indefinitely.

Lord Bauer is also dismissive of the arguments of the Brandt Report and asserts that 'Exports bought with the proceeds of foreign aid are given away.' He is opposed to any suggestion that Third World debts should be cancelled or rescheduled because such measures 'amount to preferential treatment of the incompetent, the improvident or the dishonest'. He rejects the view that Western prosperity has been achieved at the expense of the Third World and proposes that aid should only be allocated to governments that carry out 'effective administration' and pursue 'liberal economic policies'.

Aid: a view from the Left

A radical view from the left is that of Teresa Hayter, summed up in the original title of her study of the activities of the World Bank in Latin America.[10] For her, aid is imperialism. 'Aid can be explained only in terms of an attempt to preserve the capitalist system in the Third World. Aid is not a particularly effective instrument for achieving this; hence its current decline. But, in so far as it is effective, its contribution to the well-being of the people of the Third World is negative.'

Aid merely serves to facilitate 'the continuation of massive outflows of private profits and interest on past debts', and 'to create and sustain, within the Third World, a class which is dependent on the continued existence of aid and private investment and which, therefore, becomes an ally of imperialism'.[11] More recently (with

10. Hayter, T., *Aid as Imperialism*, Penguin Books, 1971.
11. ibid., p. 9.

Catharine Watson),[12] and responding to Lord Bauer, she develops the argument that aid is highly politically biased towards those countries that adopt a favourable attitude to the interests of Western private foreign investment. In particular, the World Bank and the International Monetary Fund are criticized as 'prepared to be lenient towards corrupt, inefficient and frequently brutal right-wing governments that are of economic and strategic importance to the West', while 'In general, the Bank finds it difficult to deal with the very poor, for the simple reason that they have no money, and the Bank doesn't like government subsidies.'

Also focusing on Latin America, a less extreme critic, Keith Griffin, has concluded that: 'There is absolutely no support for the orthodox view that foreign aid accelerates the rate of growth.' Indeed, he argues, it can frequently be retarding in its effects. Aid, embodying western technology, can lead to a wastefully high capital–output ratio. 'Foreign savings often tend to supplant rather than supplement (let alone increase) domestic savings.'[13] And 'foreign investors may leave domestic entrepreneurs on the margin of economic activity; they may pre-empt the most profitable opportunities and retard the development of an investing class. Should the presence of investment from economically advanced societies frustrate the growth of an indigenous entrepreneurial group, the chances for long-run development will be seriously prejudiced.'[14]

In contrast to Bauer, Griffin sees as a disadvantage of public aid its use as a lever to persuade less developed countries to accept private foreign capital – with a consequent 'bias in favour of private enterprise'.

The differences in the positions of these right- and left-wing critics of foreign aid are very obvious. Bauer believes in the efficacy of free market forces – both internally and externally, ignoring the imperfections and distributional effects consequent upon an initial inequality which those on the left will heavily emphasize as the rationale of deliberately interventionist policies. But what is perhaps more interesting is the extent to which they agree.

12. Hayter, T., and Watson, C., *Aid, Rhetoric and Reality*, Pluto Press, London, 1985.

13. Griffin, K., *Underdevelopment in Spanish America*, Allen & Unwin, 1969, pp. 121, 122.

14. ibid., p. 125.

Both are highly sceptical about the effectiveness of aid pro-grammes as they have so far operated in promoting economic development. Both argue that its effects have often been retarding rather than expansionary. Both question the dominant role of capital which has often been implied in aid programmes and, above all, both stress that development must ultimately be an indigenous process and that foreign capital imports can sap rather than reinforce the development drive.

Thus, for Bauer, 'What matters overwhelmingly is people's faculties, attitudes, motivations and institutions. I do not like the idea behind so much discussion that the salvation of these countries depends on us, that we do something to them. I like to think that it depends on the people themselves, whether they want material progress in the sense that they are prepared to give up the attitudes, customs, motivations and institutions which obstruct material progress. I think external factors are marginal.'[15]

And, for Griffin too, the 'development process requires a strong ideological foundation – whether this be nationalism, communism, or Catholic socialism. . . . Foreign investment, however, is not the type of activity which generates and sustains an ideological fervour; this is something which only domestic efforts can produce.'[16]

There is no doubt that foreign aid has frequently been used by recipient countries as an easy substitute for the painful decisions and policies involved in the generation of genuine domestic devel-opment, and that aid itself – motivated by donor considerations other than promoting economic development – has served to postpone the beginnings of the development process.

Two questions arise. To what extent *could* aid programmes be reformulated to provide genuine development assistance? And what are the continuing obstacles to development which exist, apart from aid considerations, in the poor countries themselves? These are questions to which we now turn.

15. Bauer, P., House of Commons Select Committee on Overseas Aid, Session 1969–70, op. cit.
16. Griffin, op. cit., p. 132.

PART FIVE
HOW MANY WORLDS?

1. The great divide

One of the aims of this book is to emphasize just how great is the present divide between the Rich World and the Poor World. The frightening extent of the development gap is difficult to over-stress, and yet it is a fact of which people in affluent societies still seem only vaguely aware. It is a division which must first of all be viewed in absolute terms. The great majority of the world's people live in poverty, barely subsisting on income levels which are so low as to be hard to imagine in western terms. In Britain we complain that growth is only 2 per cent per annum, but on a per capita income of more than £5,000 that is enough to provide a *rise* in real income of £100 per year. It is almost beyond credence that there are millions of people in Asia and other parts of the underdeveloped world who have a *total* annual income of only that amount.

It is difficult to believe that despite these appallingly low standards of material comfort the peoples of the underdeveloped countries generally achieve high levels of cultural and social contentment. Material poverty with its implications of under-nutrition, ill-health and lack of education serve only to narrow the opportunities of human development. What may in the past have appeared to western observers as contentment was more often resignation. But such fatalistic acceptance of poverty has now given way, in a world of easy communications, to a great groundswell of rising expectations.

This is not to argue that the poorer countries will, or should, ape the growth pattern of present affluent societies. Undiscerning adoption of the goal of economic growth in western countries – regardless of its composition, of the distribution of income, and the costs of achieving it – does not, as we should now be aware, lead to general well-being (particularly when, as recently, it is accompanied by mass unemployment). But regardless of how far they follow the path of modern economic growth, poor countries *must* make a major leap forward from their present low material standards.

Within these limitations of conscious choice, underdeveloped countries are bound to be concerned at the gap which exists between themselves and their richer counterparts. Poverty is a relative as well as an absolute concept. The present situation is that the material gap between Rich and Poor is widening. This is true both in absolute and relative terms. It has already created a state of extreme international economic inequality, and projections of present trends show the staggering degree to which this will be aggravated still further over coming decades.

What has to be clearly understood is the extent to which this process has now acquired its own momentum. The forces built into present economic mechanisms are all pushing in the direction of widening rather than narrowing economic disparities. They are forces which will divide the world in the future at an accelerating rate. The development gap is already the product of nearly two centuries of different rates of economic change in rich and poor countries. The trend towards increased international economic inequality can be halted and reversed only by deliberate and positive policies.

It should be remembered, too, that the division between Rich and Poor is broadly along racial lines. Rich is nearly always white, Poor non-white. This aspect of unequal economic advancement adds an alarming dimension to the problem of international inequality. The consequences of doing nothing to prevent the development gap from widening still farther are therefore extremely disturbing.

It is not a problem which will solve itself. Ignoring it will not make it go away. And yet how far has the urgency of the issue permeated the consciousness of the citizens and governments of rich countries? In the section on international trade, we saw how the present trade policies pursued by rich countries are nearly the mirror image of what they *would* be if governments matched their declared intention to reduce international inequalities by genuine attempts to do so. In the section on capital and labour movements, we saw how aid and investment have often served to benefit donors to a greater degree than recipients, and how their effect has been partially offset by a brain drain from poor to rich countries.

The recent scale and quality of development assistance have been quite inadequate and yet the need to actively promote the development of the Poor World is a matter to which less rather than greater priority is now being given. The American administration, for example, is anxious to scale down its commitments to multilateral aid agencies, such as the World Bank, and concentrate on bilateral aid which can more easily be directed to serve United States interests. In Britain, the Ministry set up to deal with overseas aid has once again been demoted to a department of the Foreign Office.

The fact that governments only half-heartedly pursue inadequate (and often misleadingly presented) aid policies partly reflects the underlying apathy of the voters in rich countries towards measures taken to reduce international inequality. Helping poor countries may not be a popular vote catcher but most people in industrial countries now support the principle of aid for the poor nations. Even so in times of temporary economic difficulty it is still foreign aid programmes which are the favourite objects of reduced spending by governments.

Those with easier access to an understanding of the problem show little more awareness. How to develop two thirds of the world, how to reduce massive economic disparities between nations – these are surely *the* economic problems of our time. But its importance is still not reflected in the way in which economics is commonly taught in rich countries. Development problems, if they are mentioned at all, are generally relegated to a brief passage towards the end of most standard textbooks. Development economics continues to be a 'special subject' tackled by relatively few students of economics. Such lack of perspective is ominously similar to failure elsewhere in orthodox economic thinking. During the interwar period and again today, many economists have woven intricate theories about the optimum allocation of resources achievable through the market mechanism – while leaving the unemployed millions to face the miserable realities of its failures in practice.

It is this lack of urgency in attitudes towards the development problem which is the most disturbing aspect of the present situation. It would be desperate enough if expertise and general goodwill were now being channelled on a large scale into devising appropriate measures to deal with the question of international inequality. What is alarming is that the extent of the problem does not yet seem to have been generally recognized, and that the policies which we continue to implement are ones which divide the two worlds still farther.

The costs of such blindness may prove to be enormous. In the following sections we spell out some of the more obvious ingredients in a positive policy towards world development, together with the major obstacles to them being put into effect. It is relatively easy to propose technical solutions to the problem, but very much harder to foresee that the will to implement them will be forthcoming.

2. What motivates the Rich?

Of all the reasons why rich countries should give development assistance to poor economies, the one which predominated in the immediately postwar years was the belief that economic development would provide a bulwark against the further spread of Communism. The existence of widespread poverty was seen as the seed-bed for the propagation of Marxism, with poor countries ripe for a communist take-over. Such an outcome could only be avoided by demonstrating that economic progress was possible within the capitalist framework.

This is a view which now seems astonishingly naïve – although it still has its supporters. Poverty, on the scale found in much of the underdeveloped world, generally ferments little more than apathy. The really poor lack both the energy and the initiative to bring about major political changes. It is development, by showing the possibility of change – and perhaps creating dissatisfaction at the rate of change – which is more likely to arouse interest in alternative political and social systems. In this respect, too, it must be remembered that to the people of poor countries, used to the domination of a variety of foreign and indigenous masters, 'freedoms from' may have a great deal more attraction than those 'freedoms to' which are so much cherished in more affluent societies. Life in some of the more regimented planned economies may have little appeal for those brought up in rich, liberal western countries; but if our interest is in promoting international development rather than a narrow defence of capitalism, then the genuine contributions which can be made by such regimes to economic development must be recognized. There remains something of a taboo in western writing on development on studying and learning from their efforts.

The old Cold War rationale for development assistance has become more sophisticated with the years. But political considerations still frequently dictate how much help should be given, in what form and to whom. Aid is often regarded as the price which has to be paid for supporting regimes which accord more or less with the political or economic values of the donors, or as an instrument for securing protection of its strategic interests. Paul Streeten once gave the following cynical advice to would-be recipients: 'If you wish to maximize the aid received per head of your population, you must become a very small country. If you are a member of a federation, break away. If you have an irredentist movement, encourage it. You must register a low temperature in the Cold War, belong to NATO, CENTO, SEATO and as many other military pacts as possible. You must have a regime that *declares* that it is favourable to private enterprise. The fact that the public sector is in fact much larger in the countries that preach the virtues of private investment than it is in yours is quite irrelevant.'[1]

1. Streeten, P., 'A Poor Nation's Guide to Getting Aid', *New Society*, 1968.

Add to all these qualities a common frontier with a communist country, and a substantial flow of aid is assured.

It is not merely that trying to buy friends and influence political policy through aid has often proved counter-productive. Much more important, from our present standpoint, is that short-term political interest may seriously conflict with the needs of long-term development. Support of corrupt regimes may benefit the donor while strengthening groups in recipient countries who have a vested interest against economic change.

A second set of motives lurking behind aid giving is that it is often in the economic interest of the donor countries. The report of the Independent Commission on International Development Issues, *North–South: A Programme for Survival*, argued in 1980 that there was a mutuality of interest for both the industrial nations of the North and the underdeveloped countries of the South in promoting development. The Commission consisted of out of office politicians from both North and South and was chaired by the former chancellor of West Germany, Herr Willy Brandt. The Brandt Report, as it is better known, examined the problems of Third World poverty, the then high oil prices, growing trade protectionism and high levels of arms spending. The report warned that failure to tackle these problems would both deepen poverty in the South and lead to recession in the North. In particular the Commission recommended massive transfers of resources to underdeveloped countries, agreement on oil prices and reform of the international trading system. In the event few heeded the warnings of the Brandt Report, the world slumped into economic recession and market forces reduced petroleum prices.

However the Brandt Report remains one of the clearest statements of the self-interest argument for foreign aid. A massive transfer of resources (equivalent to the Marshall Plan for western Europe at the end of the Second World War) made through bi-lateral aid programmes, institutions like the World Bank and by increasing the liquidity of the International Monetary Fund should stimulate economic growth in the underdeveloped South and create orders for goods and services from the industrial North. This revitalized economic activity in the industrial nations should in turn lead to greater demand for imports from the Third World. 'The South cannot grow adequately without the North. The North cannot prosper or improve its situation unless there is greater progress in the South.'[2] But even this more encouragingly expansionist approach to world development does not explain is how the development gap between North and South is ever to be bridged.

In practice governments mistrust theories that Third World development will benefit everyone, fearing that new orders and jobs will go to neighbouring countries and not to their own nation. Most government aid is therefore tied to the purchase of goods and services in the donor country, even though it may be cheaper for the underdeveloped country to buy locally or from a third nation. Tying ensures that jobs are created in the donor country but reduces the value of the aid to the recipient. In 1983 three quarters of Britain's bilateral aid was spent on British goods and services, for example. Indeed the Overseas Development Administration (ODA) estimated that British goods and services equivalent to 120 per cent of the country's multilateral aid were purchased by the international aid agencies.[3]

There are a number of criteria for spending Britain's overseas aid. The first, established in 1975 with the publication of the White Paper 'More Help for the Poorest' (Cmnd 3670) is that aid should be directed at the poorest countries and as far as possible, at the poorest groups within those countries. The second group of criteria, added in 1980, is that aid should also satisfy 'political, industrial and commercial considerations'.[4] This enables the Government to concentrate aid on friendly regimes and deny aid to others. It also formally acknowledges that aid may be allocated, at least in part, to provide orders for British companies and jobs for British workers. Part of the aid budget, the Aid-Trade Provision, is used to subsidize companies wanting to win orders in the Third World, as long as it can be argued that the project has some development value. In 1984 8 per cent of Britain's bilateral aid was spent on ATP projects. Other aid donors allocate their aid along similar lines. On bank loans and private investment the return in the form of profits, interest and dividends is, of course, even more explicit, and to the extent that aid does succeed in stimulating economic growth of underdeveloped countries, it results in an expansion of

2. *North–South: A Programme for Survival*, Pan, 1980.
3. Overseas Development Administration, *British Overseas Aid 1983*.
4. House of Commons debate, 20 February 1980.

the world economy and business which primarily benefits major traders like Britain.

Again Paul Streeten's advice to would-be aid recipients remains pertinent: 'Whenever an overseas firm comes to you for a concession – with the promise that it will raise your exports or encourage import substitution and, therefore, be splendid for your balance of payments – check carefully what story it has told the authorities guarding the foreign exchange position in its mother country. Often you will find that the very same firm received permission to spend some money abroad on the ground that the investment would strengthen the balance of payments of the capital-exporting country. The same firm that promises to export more from Britain may also promise *you* to import less from Britain ... *Always look a gift horse in the mouth* ... Aid from donors' surplus capacity means that you, the Poor, are helping to reduce unemployment and to raise profits in the countries of the Rich. If you accept food aid, this helps the party in power in the donor country to keep the farm vote, sometimes at the expense of your indigenous agriculture. If you buy fertilizers, it keeps important branches of the donor's chemical industry in business. Aid-tying lets producers raise prices against you and gives them a captive market. Sending your young and promising men to be trained helps donors to staff their hospitals, factories and universities with the best of your brains.'[5]

These are the motives which in practice have largely dominated aid policies, but if aid is to do more than serve donor self-interests, if it is to help reduce international economic disparities, then it must take forms which benefit the recipient countries more than the donors themselves. But such a 'something for nothing' approach implies acceptance of a *moral* responsibility by the rich countries for the plight of the poorer three quarters before there can be any real hope that aid will serve its potentially significant role in promoting development and reducing inequalities.

There are those who emphatically deny that rich countries have such a responsibility. Professor Bauer, for instance, attacks the view of foreign aid 'as the discharge of the moral duty to help the poor' on the grounds that 'foreign aid is taxpayers' money

5. Streeten, P., 'A Poor Nation's Guide to Getting Aid', op. cit.

compulsorily collected. The payers have no choice and often do not even know that they are contributing. Foreign aid is outside the area of volition and choice, and therefore has no moral element.'[6] What this argument neglects is the fact that the taxpayers' money is 'compulsorily collected' not by an arbitrary authority but by a government which they themselves have elected. Taxation on a redistributive basis can surely be as much an expression of collective morality as private charity is of individual morality. Indeed, what evidence there is suggests that public support for aid to the under-developed countries *is* based on the moral conviction that rich countries ought to help poorer ones.[7] But *why* should they do so?

A prime reason why they should is that it is inconsistent with their values not to do so. Governments and electorates in rich countries have generally subscribed to ideals which see the elimination of poverty and inequalities as important domestic goals. Even governments which say they believe in the efficacy of the free market and dislike government (or public) spending, continue some programmes of assistance to regions of very high unemployment and make state funded payments to individuals without work. How effective these policies are is not a relevant issue here. What *is* at issue is the propriety of basing domestic and external policies on quite different sets of values. If poverty and widening inequalities are abhorrent to many people *within* this country, what is it that makes it tolerable to perpetuate and accentuate them in other parts of the world? That ideals *do* extend beyond national frontiers can be seen from the remarkable public responses to well-publicized disasters such as Ethiopia. But what still needs to be more fully understood is that the abject poverty of such peoples is a chronic condition, rather than the temporary result of some natural hazard or political crisis.

A second moral basis for aid generosity is the fact that rich countries are to some extent directly responsible for creating the present degree of international poverty. In the historical section of this book, we examined the extent to which imperialism was an important element, firstly in establishing an initial international

6. Bauer, P., House of Commons Select Committee on Overseas Aid, Session 1969–70, HMSO.
7. Gallup, 'Omnibus Report on Overseas Aid', conducted on behalf of Office of Population Censuses & Surveys, 1983.

economic inequality and secondly in widening the development gap. Our general conclusion was that if imperialism had not existed there would have been no certainty that less developed countries would at that time also have embarked on modern economic growth. Imperialism, none the less, created conditions in which it became effectively impossible for such a take-off to occur at all. And, by creating an artificial division of labour, and encouraging policies based on metropolitan self-interest, imperialism was certainly a major factor in widening still farther an initial development gap.

Underdevelopment, it is sometimes said, is the product of development. It is the fact that a handful of countries have been able to economically expand at an unprecedented rate during the last couple of centuries which has left the rest lagging behind and created the present enormous distance between nations. The degree to which this is a cumulative process, the extent to which the cards are systematically stacked in favour of the rich rather than the poorer countries is, once again, a morally persuasive argument that rich countries should accept a considerable degree of responsibility for assisting the present underdeveloped world.

These are arguments which have so far had little place on the political platform. Until they have, it may well be the case that aid is bound to be channelled along the self-interested lines which have already been described – and supported only reluctantly by the elected representatives of the voters in rich countries. Gunnar Myrdal argues forcefully that 'only by appealing to people's moral feelings will it be possible to create the popular basis for increasing aid to underdeveloped countries as substantially as it is needed'. And he goes on to assert a belief that such a popular support *would* be forthcoming given the necessary publicity for the issue. 'Ordinary people in our western civilizational milieu – and they are the ones who in the final instance determine the trend of policies in our countries over the years – *can* be brought to act on the basis of feelings of compassion and solidarity, but they soon become cold toward alleged national interests, particularly when, as regularly happens, those turn out to have been spurious and misdirected. . . . It is unrealistic and self-defeating to distrust the moral forces of a nation.'[8]

8. Myrdal, G., *The Challenge of World Poverty*, pp. 356–7.

The former West German chancellor in his introduction to the Brandt Report put it this way: 'Mankind has never before had such ample technical and financial resources for coping with hunger and poverty. The immense task can be tackled once the necessary collective will is mobilized.' Now should be the time at which concerted efforts are made to highlight the development issue as the most urgent problem of our times. Instead, what do we find happening? On the one hand there is a depressing consensus view developing of the inefficacy of aid – 'on all sides a weariness' – which leads to fundamental questioning of the aid programmes from left- and right-wing economists in both donor and recipient countries, an over-reaction which is dangerous in neglecting the very real contribution which aid *could* play. And, on the other hand, optimistic target-setting about the future volume of aid which largely ignores the lesson from the past that the quality of aid and the forms which it takes are at least as important as its total.

3. Aid targetry

As a means of increasing the total volume of resources flowing from rich countries to poor ones, the setting of aid targets by development pressure groups may have served a useful function in 'focusing political will'. Thus in 1964 UNCTAD I proposed that advanced economies should contribute annually 1 per cent of their national incomes to aiding underdeveloped countries. The 1 per cent target was more closely defined in UNCTAD II in 1968 and by the Pearson Commission on International Development the following year (the Pearson Report was a similar initiative to the Brandt Report eleven years later). The 1 per cent target included both official government assistance and private commercial investment. Under the later definition 70 per cent of the total flow of resources should be *official* assistance, that is 0.7 per cent of GNP. The Brandt Report went further and recommended that the 0·7 per cent of GNP target should be met by 1985 and that official aid should rise to 1 per cent of GNP before the end of the twentieth century.

By 1985, of course, the target for official aid had not been met. As the Brandt Report explained, 'While the one per cent norm for overall net flows (including private investment and commercial lending) has been reached, the hopes aroused for the ODA target have been dashed.'[9] By 1983 the average level of official aid from the OECD countries was 0·36 per cent of GNP or just half the United Nations target. In 1968 it had been slightly higher at 0·39 per cent of GNP. Indeed, as far as the British case is concerned, official assistance formed a *declining* proportion of gross national income in the first half of the 1980s.

23. British net official aid flows as % of GNP	
1973–7	0·36
1979–80	0·52
1980–81	0·35
1981–2	0·43
1982–3	0·37
1983–4	0·35

Sources: Public expenditure White Papers

In 1984 Sir Geoffrey Howe, the Foreign Secretary, told the House of Commons, 'Our aid programme remains the fifth largest among industrialized countries, and the Government remains committed to maintaining a substantial aid programme.' He added that, 'Private capital flows can, and do, play a vital and increasing role for many developing countries.'[10] The British Government accepts both the overall 1 per cent of GNP target (which it points out has been met) and the 0·7 per cent target for official assistance, but it has not committed itself to meeting that secondary target by any particular date. On present trends it is very unlikely to do so in the foreseeable future.

24. British private flows (net) to developing countries as % of GNP	
1981	2·31
1982	1·29
1983	1·25

Source: Overseas Development Administration, *British Overseas Aid 1983*

9. *North–South: A Programme for Survival*, op. cit.
10. House of Commons debate, 22 November 1984.

Despite the notable lack of success in achieving the 0·7 per cent target, a third aid target was added to the United Nations armoury in 1981, at the United Nations Conference on Least Developed Countries in Paris. The second Brandt Report explained that the conference 'concluded with a commitment by most donor countries to reach a target of 0·15 per cent of GNP for the least developed countries (within the 0·7 per cent target); others would double their aid to these countries'.[11] The Least Developed are a group of some 36 of the poorest countries in the world, most of which are in the continent of Africa. The United Nations believes they merit special attention because of their extreme poverty and because they generally do not attract private investment or commercial loans. The British Government has not committed itself to the 0·15 per cent target, believing the boundaries of the Least Developed to be too tightly drawn. India, for example, a major recipient of British Aid, is excluded from the UN definition, although Bangladesh is classified as a Least Developed Country.

Apart from official government aid, of course, there is also private commercial investment by multinational companies and banks. The Brandt Report argued that 'A very substantial mutual interest lies in harnessing the economic strength and experience of the multinationals for development.'[12] It went on to propose an improved framework for investment in developing countries. 'Home countries should not restrict investment or the transfer of technology abroad, and should desist from other restrictive practices such as export controls or market allocation agreements. Host countries in turn should not restrict current transfers such as profits, royalties and dividends, or the repatriation of capital, so long as they are on terms which were agreed.'[13] The Commissioners recognized the sovereign right of countries to nationalize the assets of foreign companies, but sought fair compensation. They accepted that 'Multinational corporations have also been heavily criticized for unethical political and commercial activities,' but their report stated: 'This is not to suggest that as a class transnational corpor-

11. *Common Crisis: North–South Co-operation for World Recovery*, The Brandt Commission, Pan, 1983.
12. *North–South: A Programme for Survival*, op. cit. p. 73.
13. ibid., p. 192.

ations have been guilty of such practices.'[14] But is private investment from overseas likely to help developing countries?

Development, as we have stressed throughout, is a process
of basic structural change involving fundamental redirection of
attitudes and institutions. The stimulation of indigenous entrepreneurship, emphasis on rural development, moves towards increased equality and regional balance, promotion of more
appropriate technologies, the inculcation of a development ideology – these are crucial steps towards development. But to private
investors, they are all too likely to appear as evidence of dangerous
instability. The fact is that those countries which are most successful
in creating a development-oriented environment are probably the
ones which will find it most difficult to encourage a flow of capital
imports. (Indeed, in all probability, it is these which are anyway
least likely to want such dependence.)

Private capital is less venturesome than is sometimes suggested.
In Britain, capital does not flow freely to Northern Ireland or other
relatively less prosperous regions in order to take advantage of
greater labour availability there. It follows other successful capital
into already proven fields of investment. Similarly, on the international scale, private capital goes to countries where favourable
terms are offered and in which stability can be guaranteed, and
particularly into exploitation of mineral resources where dependence on local co-operation is minimized.

It was fully recognized in the Brandt Report that 'Foreign
investment has moved to a limited number of developing countries,
mainly those which could offer political stability and a convenient
economic environment, including tax incentives, large markets,
cheap labour and easy access to oil or other natural resources.'[15]
But the Commissioners then failed to draw the obvious conclusion –
that the contribution of private capital in promoting economic
development is therefore a limited and dubious one. The inherent
conflict which exists between the conditions created by energetic
development policies and those necessary to attract private capital
apparently escaped them.

14. ibid., p. 188.
15. ibid., p. 187.

4. The anti-developers

Development has been defined throughout as a fundamental change in basic attitudes and institutions, in which the mass of the population are involved, and which enhances the possibility that the objectives of the society will be achieved. Since such objectives are commonly, but not exclusively, expressed in material terms, this implies that development ultimately results in a faster rate of growth – although it should not be equated with it.

In preceding sections, some possible ingredients of the process have been outlined – land reform, rural development, radical educational re-structuring, selectivity with regard to accepting aid, new trade outlooks, greater emphasis on income equality and social justice. Admittedly, this is only one set of prescriptions. There may be many paths to development. But why, in a world of increasing international economic disparity, are so many poor countries failing to develop, by any route? Is there some basic blockage to development which we have so far overlooked?

The American economist Paul Baran, writing in 1952, was quite sure that there was. The technical means of solving the problem of underdevelopment were, he felt, relatively straightforward. The problem lay in the nature of the social order – which made it very unlikely that the policies needed for development would ever be introduced and implemented. The crucial obstacle to development, for him, was the fact that 'The economic and political order maintained by the ruling coalition of owning classes finds itself invariably at odds with all the urgent needs of the underdeveloped economies. Neither the social fabric that it embodies nor the institutions that rest upon it are conducive to progressive economic development.'[16]

'Mechanically', he said, 'it would appear indeed that much could be done, by a well-advised regime in an underdeveloped country, to provide for a relatively rapid increase of total output, accompanied by an improvement of the living standards of the

16. Baran, P. A., *On the Political Economy of Backwardness*, The Manchester School, January 1952. References are to the reprinted version in *The Economics of Underdevelopment*, eds. Agarwala, A. N., and Singh, S. P., Galaxy Books, New York: OUP, 1958, p. 80.

population.[17] Progressive taxation and capital levies could siphon off a surplus to be applied to productive investment; the State should direct its investment into essential infrastructure; technical schools and wider educational opportunities should be introduced; the government must step in to undertake investment where the social benefit is high but private gain little; the State should stabilize inflation, counteract the effects on the production and consumption patterns of extreme income inequalities, and render capital flight impossible.

'But', he gloomily concluded, 'the mere listing of the steps that would have to be undertaken, in order to ensure an expansion of output and income in an underdeveloped country, reveals the utter implausibility of the view that they could be carried out by the governments existing in most underdeveloped countries ... The crucial fact rendering the realization of a developmental pro-gramme illusory is the political and social structure of the govern-ments in power.'

This is because they have a deeply entrenched interest *against* development. 'The alliance of property-owning classes controlling the destinies of most underdeveloped countries cannot be expected to design and to execute a set of measures running counter to each and all of their immediate vested interests.'[18] Those in power, he argues, 'are those who benefit most from the *status quo* – politically, socially, economically. It is no good expecting those who enjoy the benefits of the present system to bring about fundamental changes in it.'

And even if, he went on to argue, 'To appease the restive public, blueprints of progressive measures are officially announced, their enforcement is wilfully sabotaged ... And even if (they) could be enforced by the corrupt officials operating in the demoralized business communities of underdeveloped countries, such enforce-ment would to a large extent defeat its original purpose.'[19] This is because where there is only a profit motive a 'taxation system succeeding in confiscating large parts of these profits is bound to kill off private investment'. And 'Where the only stimulus to hard work on the part of intellectuals, technicians and civil servants is

17. ibid., p. 86.
18. ibid., p. 88.
19. ibid., p. 89.

the chance of partaking in the privileges of the ruling class, a policy aimed at the reduction of inequality of social status is bound to smother effort. The injection of planning into a society living in the twilight between feudalism and capitalism cannot but result in additional corruption, larger and more artful evasions of the law, and more brazen abuses of authority. There would seem to be no exit from the impasse.'[20]

For Baran the exit lay in violent revolution ... 'abrupt and painful. The land not given to the peasants legally may be taken by them forcibly. High incomes not confiscated through taxation may be eliminated by outright expropriation. Corrupt officials not retired in orderly fashion may be removed by violent action.'[21]

This was a Marxist view expressed in the early fifties. The experience of the underdeveloped countries during the past twenty years confirms rather than refutes the view that the existence of deeply entrenched elitist groups represents a powerful anti-development interest. Baran's ideas, when he first put them forward, might have been dismissed by most western writers on development as the fundamentalist dogmatism of a political extremist. But this is no longer the case. Increasingly, those interested in the problems of economic development have become aware that those in power in many underdeveloped countries may *not* be motivated by the desire to actively promote development as we have been defining it.

Professor Gunnar Myrdal, the Swedish economist, is a very different political animal from Baran. He is an ex-Minister of the Swedish government, international administrator, and one of the most eminent of contemporary economists. He is certainly no Marxist. On the contrary, as a self-described 'student in the great liberal tradition of the Enlightenment', he finds it 'a hateful experience to be driven to the conclusion that the awakening of the masses and their becoming conscious of their interests and prepared to fight for the radical reforms needed for development shall happen in a world political constellation where they shall find themselves projected into a movement of national communism'.[22]

And yet, in his book, *The Challenge of World Poverty*, Myrdal

20. ibid.
21. ibid., p. 90.
22. Myrdal, G., op. cit., p. 435.

again and again stresses the degree to which elitism is the major
obstacle to economic development. He identifies all the underdeveloped countries as being more or less *soft states*, the term being
understood 'to comprise all the various types of social indiscipline
... The laxity and arbitrariness in a national community that can
be characterized as a soft state can be, and are, *exploited for personal
gain by people who have economic, social and political power*.'[23]
Thus, for example, vital land reform and taxation laws on income
and wealth are thwarted because '*if they were strictly formulated
and effectively implemented, they would have effects on social and
economic stratification*. But exactly for this reason tremendous
vested interests are mobilized to emasculate them.'[24] The reason
that the soft state impedes development is fundamentally due to
the fact that 'all the power is in the hands of the upper class who
can afford egalitarian laws and policy but are in an unchallenged
position to prevent their implementation'.[25]

But is their position so impregnable? After all, the postwar period
has witnessed countless examples of apparently powerful regimes
being overthrown and replaced. For Myrdal, however, such coups
imply nothing more than a 'reshuffling of power among the various
upper-class groups, usually manoeuvred by higher military officers
grasping and thereafter holding on to a measure of monopoly of
power. Power is, however, always shared to different degrees with
other upper-class groups.'[26]

Nor does Myrdal see any great prospect of widespread revolution
from below because the 'masses are mostly passive, apathetic and
inarticulate'.[27] They 'are the object of politics but hardly anywhere
its subject. They are ruled by compromises, accommodation and
sometimes infighting among the various groups that together
constitute the upper-class ...'[28] And when he asks, 'Is there a
limit to the misery human beings can bear without revolt-
ing?' he is forced to the appalling conclusion that 'The utterly
miserable living conditions quietly endured by many in the rural

23. ibid., p. 207.
24. ibid., p. 221.
25. ibid., p. 222.
26. ibid., p. 64.
27. ibid., p. 62.
28. ibid., p. 63.

and urban slums today would suggest that there is no such limit'.[29]

These lengthy quotations illustrate a remarkable unanimity between development experts working from very different political premises. Marxist and western liberal both stress that it is not so much ignorance of the technical means as a lack of political will which is the crucial obstacle to development. In discussing the various changes needed in poor countries, we tend to assume that their governments have development as their prime policy objective. It is that assumption that Baran and Myrdal question, arguing that the power structure in underdeveloped countries is such that those with the ability to implement radical reforms have interests which profoundly bias them against doing so.

There is another assumption commonly made which is even more tragically questionable. Part of the ethos of developed countries is an optimism which appears justified by their experience to date that all problems are soluble by rational human ordering. But Myrdal, on the other hand, faces up to the fact that in India or the larger part of South Asia, for example, 'there is quite clearly a possibility or even perhaps a probability that ... there will be neither much evolution nor revolution ...'[30] There is, in fact, a 'possibility of utter and increasing impoverishment'.[31]

5. Believing in development

So much of what has passed as development during recent decades is nothing of the sort – if development connotes mass involvement in a structural transformation of the economic and social system. In part, the steps towards development have been so faltering because of real controversy about its mechanisms. Economists initially exaggerated the manipulation of a key economic variable, such as investment, as the way of bringing about the desired results. The limitations of this western approach have been increasingly exposed; and development strategists today recognize that the attack on underdevelopment must be on a broad front and penetrate the whole social fabric. However, the general recognition of

29. ibid., p. 432.
30. ibid., p. 431.
31. ibid., p. 432.

the importance of fundamental changes such as land reform, the need for rural development, radical educational change and the role of intermediate technology, has not sufficed to ensure their implementation. We have just been suggesting that the existence of elitist groups with deeply anti-development interests is one major obstacle to change. Another factor impeding development is lack of a general commitment to the idea of change.

Development *has* taken place in a handful of instances during the postwar period. The list is a short one, and contentious. Often-quoted examples are Taiwan and South Korea, on the one hand; and on the other, China, Cuba and North Korea. It is a list which suggests that there are still alternative paths to quite different sorts of development. One is the Communist course, in which individual freedoms are in many ways restricted but which results in a widening of horizons for the general mass of people. The other, more similar to that plotted by the earlier developers, is essentially capitalistic and inegalitarian.

What they have in common – and this is what marks them off from cases of non-development – is that they are based on a development ideology which has caught hold of, and involved, the great mass of people. It is this essential ingredient in the development process which is stressed by Professor David McClelland of Harvard University when he argues: 'There is no real substitute for ideological fervour ... Ideological movements of all sorts are an important source of the emotional fervour needed to convert people to new norms. They are necessary and should be supported in whatever form is politically feasible or most congenial to the country concerned.'[32]

One possible basis for such an 'urge to improve' is newly won political independence. Throwing off the shackles of colonial rule can certainly conduce to the creation of an atmosphere in which everything is seen to be possible and from which past constraints on progress have been removed. This was the stimulus towards development efforts which impelled many underdeveloped countries in the years after the Second World War. However, it has not generally proved to be a sufficient impetus, and there are three main reasons for this. The first is that the ruling groups which took

32. Quoted in Griffin, K., *Underdevelopment in Spanish America*, p. 132.

control on withdrawal of the metropolitan powers consisted of those who had been deeply involved in the freedom struggle. Unfortunately, the qualities required in successful leaders in the fight for independence do not necessarily coincide with those demanded in vigorous development strategists – for whom lengthy stretches in British prisons may not be the most appropriate apprenticeship. Instead of destroying the privileges previously enjoyed by their colonial rulers, such leaders have too often preferred to inherit them. Secondly, the existence of a background of imperial domination has often served to weaken the development thrust by providing a scapegoat for continuing failures. It has often been easy to cast blame on the dead hand of the past as a substitute for effective action now. And thirdly, independence fervour has proved difficult to sustain as a base for the prolonged struggle for economic development.

Nationalism, too, has at times served as a development ideology. The threat of external aggression or the wish to assert dominance over other countries have both been used as an instrument for mobilizing energies and bringing about basic changes. The problem is that such efforts are largely channelled into non-productive activities which do little to create a long-term development base, and nationalism has also proved difficult to sustain.

Economic acquisitiveness is yet another possible source of development fervour. The impulse to make money certainly served in western countries as a powerful stimulus for individuals to seize business opportunities in ways which led to the economic expansion of those societies. But for developing countries the problem is how to artificially create those conditions which occurred spontaneously in the early developers. It has taken, in the case of countries like those listed earlier – South Korea and Taiwan – injections of American capital on a massive 'overkill' scale to engineer such opportunities, and in such situations the cost of achieving economic advancement must be measured in terms of the loss of cultural identity which has been involved.

Finally, there are the many variants of socialism on which to base a development ideology. Mass participation in the process of change in creating a society with radically different values has certainly been effective in bringing about fundamental alterations in a number of societies. Once again, however, the problem has been of how to keep up the development drive; there is a need for constant regeneration of ideological fervour.

What does seem clear is that a powerful underlying ideology is a necessary, if not sufficient, condition for development. It is those countries lacking such an ideology – which comprise the majority in the underdeveloped world – which have been least successful in promoting the necessary changes in the postwar period.

The ideology may be indigenous or it may be imported. And, as has already been stressed, depending on its nature, very different types of development can result. Choice between alternative development paths is a matter of value judgement. In this respect we should distinguish carefully between those sorts of development which *we* find attractive or obnoxious – and the situation as it appears to the inhabitants of very poor societies. *If* our concern about underdevelopment is principally because it results in intolerable poverty and inequalities, then that human aspect should be of transcending importance. Development which helps to reduce inequalities and to improve the lot of the mass of people must be welcomed whatever the political hue of the regimes under which it occurs. To repeat McClelland's phrase, ideologies conducive to development 'should be supported in whatever form is politically feasible or most congenial to the country concerned'.

Western democratic governments, when they are called upon for development assistance, certainly have the right to try to promote a type of development which accords with their own values. The use of 'leverage' has, however, often proved to be counterproductive; it can have the effect, as in the case of Nicaragua, of creating a 'resentful nationalism' which leads underdeveloped countries to seek solutions elsewhere. Then again, if the western path of development is to be seen as a genuine alternative, it must be shown to work. For the moment, its credibility is suspect. There are many grounds for doubting whether market mechanisms are an appropriate vehicle for development, and the international framework created by rich countries, as we have seen, is one in which the odds are heavily loaded against poorer nations and which works to widen rather than to narrow present inequalities. Aid, which should be channelled to those governments actively promoting development policies, all too frequently bolsters anti-development interests instead. 'Governments which facilitate foreign private investment are especially popular with donors – yet often these are precisely the ones which check, or fail to foster, social change. They also tend to be governments which fail even to control the outflow of private capital. Yet aid helps to keep them in office; on the other hand, the knowledge that political parties or leaders who oppose foreign investment and favour (e.g.) genuine land reform are ineligible for aid from some sources may affect their chances of getting or keeping power.'[33]

Readers may find that the tone of many development writers is distinctly radical. This is bound to be so, given an awareness of the frightful dimensions of the development problem. The problems of underdeveloped countries are chronic – because of both the deep-rooted nature of internal blockages to development, and the unsympathetic international framework within which solutions have to be found. The changes needed to deal with such problems are correspondingly fundamental. Either they will be made within political systems very different from our own, or our own attitudes and policies must be basically reorientated to match practice with promises. Or the problems may not be solved at all. These are the alternative scenarios for the crucial decades which lie ahead.

IT IS POSSIBLE that rich western countries, disillusioned by the failure of their policies to achieve politically favourable results in the underdeveloped world, will become increasingly withdrawn. It is certainly arguable that they have now reached positions of economic strength in which they are only marginally dependent on poor countries. They are themselves major primary producers of a variety of strategic materials; and they increasingly have the technological capability to create synthetic substitutes for those which for the time being they continue to import. As for markets for their constantly expanding output, they can depend largely on taking in each other's washing – exchanging sophisticated consumer goods within exclusive regional trading blocs. External demand is not a necessary condition for their continuing affluence when there are outlets for increased production in the form, for example, of space programmes.

And if meanwhile the 'sullen dissatisfaction' of the masses

33. Seers, D., 'The Total Relationship', *Development in a Divided World*, p. 343.

in poor countries fails to express itself in heightened political consciousness, the way is open there for the perpetual consolidations of power in the hands of corrupt self-interested groups. Régimes will change, counter-coups will follow coups without materially altering the underlying distribution of power.

With the failure of development to stem from either evolutionary or revolutionary processes, poor countries may become increasingly isolated and dispensable. Relatively, they will become more and more impoverished – and, in many cases, their absolute poverty will also grow as the Malthusian bogey of population pressure finally comes home to roost.

Slowly, apathetically, miserably, they will sink into oblivion – not with a bang but a whimper ...

IT IS POSSIBLE that events may take a more violent turn. Perhaps the forces of education and awareness of affluence elsewhere brought about by modern communications have already unleashed a growing consciousness in the masses of the poor world of the inequity of their situation. Unaided, impoverished by generations of exploitation, their frustration in failing to develop may be increasingly directed against the Rich Few. The way would be open for the nightmare portrayed by Myrdal in this way: 'If it is difficult to awaken the masses, it is also difficult to calm them down when once awakened. They cannot all be killed or imprisoned for ever.' And for Myrdal there are alarming racialist aspects to the problem: the 'development of anti-White and anti-Western emotions in some underdeveloped nations, experiencing an onslaught of white military and police forces and seeing this backed by western solidarity, tends to spread to other underdeveloped countries that are largely non-white ... It is a frightening prospect to have to fear that the relations between developed and underdeveloped countries will become infested with the colour complex ...'[34]

IT IS POSSIBLE that poor countries, sceptical about the genuineness of western assistance and policies, but having reached a stage of development at which the masses are aroused, are gradually absorbed into the communist camp. Under such régimes they may

34. Myrdal, G., op. cit., p. 434.

or may not be successful in achieving development. But what meanwhile would be the reaction of western countries? Would they be prepared to bridge the gap between the two systems? Or would they see it as an increasing threat to be resisted through military maintenance of non-communist régimes, the rationale for mounting programmes of military expenditure and the further intensification of East–West conflict . . .?

IT IS POSSIBLE that forces will grow in western countries – whether they stem from enlightened self-interest or from altruistic concern about the extent of world poverty and inequalities – which cause governments radically to reformulate the scope and nature of their present policies towards less developed countries. Such an outcome could only result from a general awareness of the dimensions of the development problem to a far greater extent than hitherto. It would require the provision of assistance from rich countries on a scale and of a *quality* which would be dictated by the *needs* of the recipients rather than the short-term advantage of the donors. It would require a fundamental re-examination of the whole gamut of Rich–Poor relationships – with regard to aid, private capital flows and ownership, trade and labour migration – to see how they could be restructured to narrow the development gap.

For this above all would be the crux of the matter: to design policies with the aim, not of improving the economic position of the developed nations, or of fighting off Communism, but of creating the prerequisites for development regardless of the political direction in which developing countries subsequently choose to move.

The postwar period has been one in which the developed countries have mostly pursued policies aimed at eliminating poverty and preventing grosser inequalities between individuals and regions from emerging within their own societies. In recent years, that concern has been less evident.

IT IS POSSIBLE that only when we again learn to show greater compassion towards the poorer and weaker members of our own communities that rich nations will take the logical leap forward in extending their moral concern to those in poor countries.

IT IS JUST POSSIBLE that Tolstoy was wrong when he declared that the rich would do anything for the poor except get off their backs.

INDEX

FOR THE BEST IN PAPERBACKS, LOOK FOR THE

In every corner of the world, on every subject under the sun, Penguin represents quality and variety – the very best in publishing today.

For complete information about books available from Penguin – including Pelicans, Puffins, Peregrines and Penguin Classics – and how to order them, write to us at the appropriate address below. Please note that for copyright reasons the selection of books varies from country to country.

In the United Kingdom: Please write to *Dept E.P., Penguin Books Ltd, Harmondsworth, Middlesex, UB7 0DA*

If you have any difficulty in obtaining a title, please send your order with the correct money, plus ten per cent for postage and packaging, to *PO Box No 11, West Drayton, Middlesex*

In the United States: Please write to *Dept BA, Penguin, 299 Murray Hill Parkway, East Rutherford, New Jersey 07073*

In Canada: Please write to *Penguin Books Canada Ltd, 2801 John Street, Markham, Ontario L3R 1B4*

In Australia: Please write to the *Marketing Department, Penguin Books Australia Ltd, P.O. Box 257, Ringwood, Victoria 3134*

In New Zealand: Please write to the *Marketing Department, Penguin Books (NZ) Ltd, Private Bag, Takapuna, Auckland 9*

In India: Please write to *Penguin Overseas Ltd, 706 Eros Apartments, 56 Nehru Place, New Delhi, 110019*

In Holland: Please write to *Penguin Books Nederland B.V., Postbus 195, NL–1380AD Weesp, Netherlands*

In Germany: Please write to *Penguin Books Ltd, Friedrichstrasse 10–12, D–6000 Frankfurt Main 1, Federal Republic of Germany*

In Spain: Please write to *Longman Penguin España, Calle San Nicolas 15, E–28013 Madrid, Spain*

In France: Please write to *Penguin Books Ltd, 39 Rue de Montmorency, F-75003, Paris, France*

In Japan: Please write to *Longman Penguin Japan Co Ltd, Yamaguchi Building, 2–12–9 Kanda Jimbocho, Chiyoda-Ku, Tokyo 101, Japan*

A CHOICE OF PENGUINS

A Question of Economics   Peter Donaldson

Twenty key issues – the City, trade unions, 'free market forces' and many others – are presented clearly and fully in this major book based on a television series.

The Economist Economics   Rupert Pennant-Rea and Clive Crook

Based on a series of 'briefs' published in the *Economist* in 1984, this important new book makes the key issues of contemporary economic thinking accessible to the general reader.

The Tyranny of the Status Quo   Milton and Rose Friedman

Despite the rhetoric, big government has actually *grown* under Reagan and Thatcher. The Friedmans consider why this is – and what we can do now to change it.

Business Wargames   Barrie G. James

Successful companies use military strategy to win. Barrie James shows how – and draws some vital lessons for today's manager.

Atlas of Management Thinking   Edward de Bono

This fascinating book provides a vital repertoire of non-verbal images – to help activate the right side of any manager's brain.

The Winning Streak   Walter Goldsmith and David Clutterbuck

A brilliant analysis of what Britain's best-run and successful companies have in common – a must for all managers.

Lateral Thinking for Management   Edward de Bono

Creativity and lateral thinking can work together for managers in developing new products or ideas; Edward de Bono shows how.

Understanding Organizations   Charles B. Handy

Of practical as well as theoretical interest, this book shows how general concepts can help solve specific organizational problems.

The Art of Japanese Management   Richard Tanner Pascale and Anthony G. Athos   With an Introduction by Sir Peter Parker

Japanese industrial success owes much to Japanese management techniques, which we in the West neglect at our peril. The lessons are set out in this important book.

My Years with General Motors   Alfred P. Sloan   With an Introduction by John Egan

A business classic by the man who took General Motors to the top – and kept them there for decades.

Introducing Management   Ken Elliott and Peter Lawrence (eds.)

An important and comprehensive collection of texts on modern management which draw some provocative conclusions.

English Culture and the Decline of the Industrial Spirit   Martin J. Wiener

A major analysis of why the 'world's first industrial nation has never been comfortable with industrialism'. 'Very persuasive' – Anthony Sampson in the *Observer*

A CHOICE OF PENGUINS

Dinosaur and Co Tom Lloyd

A lively and optimistic survey of a new breed of businessmen who are breaking away from huge companies to form dynamic enterprises in microelectronics, biotechnology and other developing areas.

The Money Machine: How the City Works Philip Coggan

How are the big deals made? Which are the institutions that *really* matter? What causes the pound to rise or interest rates to fall? This book provides clear and concise answers to these and many other money-related questions.

Parkinson's Law C. Northcote Parkinson

'Work expands so as to fill the time available for its completion': that law underlies this 'extraordinarily funny and witty book' (Stephen Potter in the *Sunday Times*) which also makes some painfully serious points for those in business or the Civil Service.

Debt and Danger Harold Lever and Christopher Huhne

The international debt crisis was brought about by Western bankers in search of quick profit and is now one of our most pressing problems. This book looks at the background and shows what we must do to avoid disaster.

Lloyd's Bank Tax Guide 1988/9

Cut through the complexities! Work the system in *your* favour! Don't pay a penny more than you have to! Written for anyone who has to deal with personal tax, this up-to-date and concise new handbook includes all the important changes in this year's budget.

The Spirit of Enterprise George Gilder

A lucidly written and excitingly argued defence of capitalism and the role of the entrepreneur within it.

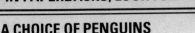
A CHOICE OF PENGUINS

Metamagical Themas   Douglas R. Hofstadter

A new mind-bending bestseller by the author of *Gödel, Escher, Bach*.

The Body   Anthony Smith

A completely updated edition of the well-known book by the author of *The Mind*. The clear and comprehensive text deals with everything from sex to the skeleton, sleep to the senses.

How to Lie with Statistics   Darrell Huff

A classic introduction to the ways statistics can be used to prove *anything*, the book is both informative and 'wildly funny' – *Evening News*

The Penguin Dictionary of Computers   Anthony Chandor and others

An invaluable glossary of over 300 words, from 'aberration' to 'zoom' by way of 'crippled lead-frog tests' and 'output bus drivers'.

The Cosmic Code   Heinz R. Pagels

Tracing the historical development of quantum physics, the author describes the baffling and seemingly lawless world of leptons, hadrons, gluons and quarks and provides a lucid and exciting guide for the layman to the world of infinitesimal particles.

The Blind Watchmaker   Richard Dawkins

'Richard Dawkins has updated evolution' – *The Times* 'An enchantingly witty and persuasive neo-Darwinist attack on the anti-evolutionists, pleasurably intelligible to the scientifically illiterate' – Hermione Lee in Books of the Year, *Observer*

Genetic Engineering for Almost Everybody   William Bains

Now that the 'genetic engineering revolution' has most certainly arrived, we all need to understand the ethical and practical implications of genetic engineering. Written in accessible language, they are set out in this major new book.

Brighter than a Thousand Suns   Robert Jungk

'By far the most interesting historical work on the atomic bomb I know of' – C. P. Snow

Turing's Man   J. David Bolter

We live today in a computer age, which has meant some startling changes in the ways we understand freedom, creativity and language. This·major book looks at the implications.

Einstein's Universe   Nigel Calder

'A valuable contribution to the de-mystification of relativity' – *Nature*

The Creative Computer   Donald R. Michie and Rory Johnston

Computers *can* create the new knowledge we need to solve some of our most pressing human problems; this path-breaking book shows how.

Only One Earth   Barbara Ward and Rene Dubos

An extraordinary document which explains with eloquence and passion how we should go about 'the care and maintenance of a small planet'.

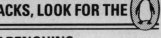

A CHOICE OF PENGUINS

The Apartheid Handbook   Roger Omond

This book provides the essential hard information about how apartheid actually works from day to day and fills in the details behind the headlines.

The World Turned Upside Down   Christopher Hill

This classic study of radical ideas during the English Revolution 'will stand as a notable monument to . . . one of the finest historians of the present age' – *The Times Literary Supplement*

Islam in the World   Malise Ruthven

'His exposition of "the Qurenic world view" is the most convincing, and the most appealing, that I have read' – Edward Mortimer in *The Times*

The Knight, the Lady and the Priest   Georges Duby

'A very fine book' (Philippe Aries) that traces back to its medieval origin one of our most important institutions, marriage.

A Social History of England   New Edition   Asa Briggs

'A treasure house of scholarly knowledge . . . beautifully written and full of the author's love of his country, its people and its landscape' – John Keegan in the *Sunday Times*, Books of the Year

The Second World War   A J P Taylor

A brilliant and detailed illustrated history, enlivened by all Professor Taylor's customary iconoclasm and wit.

A CHOICE OF PENGUINS

Beyond the Blue Horizon Alexander Frater

The romance and excitement of the legendary Imperial Airways East-bound Empire service – the world's longest and most adventurous scheduled air route – relived fifty years later in one of the most original travel books of the decade. 'The find of the year' – *Today*

Voyage through the Antarctic Richard Adams and Ronald Lockley

Here is the true, authentic Antarctic of today, brought vividly to life by Richard Adams, author of *Watership Down*, and Ronald Lockley, the world-famous naturalist. 'A good adventure story, with a lot of information and a deal of enthusiasm for Antarctica and its animals' – *Nature*

Getting to Know the General Graham Greene

'In August 1981 my bag was packed for my fifth visit to Panama when the news came to me over the telephone of the death of General Omar Torrijos Herrera, my friend and host . . .' 'Vigorous, deeply felt, at times funny, and for Greene surprisingly frank' – *Sunday Times*

The Search for the Virus Steve Connor and Sharon Kingman

In this gripping book, two leading *New Scientist* journalists tell the remarkable story of how researchers discovered the AIDS virus and examine the links between AIDS and lifestyles. They also look at the progress being made in isolating the virus and finding a cure.

Arabian Sands Wilfred Thesiger

'In the tradition of Burton, Doughty, Lawrence, Philby and Thomas, it is, very likely, the book about Arabia to end all books about Arabia' – *Daily Telegraph*

When the Wind Blows Raymond Briggs

'A visual parable against nuclear war: all the more chilling for being in the form of a strip cartoon' – *Sunday Times* 'The most eloquent anti-Bomb statement you are likely to read' – *Daily Mail*

67 13